CATHOLIC FAMILIES SERIES

GROWING IN FAITH:
A Catholic Family Sourcebook

Edited by John Roberto

D1417400

THE WORLD OF
DON BOSCO
MULTIMEDIA

New Rochelle, New York

Catholic Families Series
Growing in Faith: A Catholic Family Sourcebook

Forthcoming Catholic Families Series:
  Families with Young Adolescents
  Families and Youth
  Rites of Passage and Rites of Growth
    and Change: A Resource Guide
  Rites of Passage and Rites of Growth
    and Change: A Family Ritual Guide
  Parenting for Faith Growth: A Parent
    Education Program
  A Partnership between Family and Parish:
    A Pastoral Plan for the Transmission
    of Faith
  Leadership Training Program for Families
    and Faith
  Media, Faith, and the Family: A Catalog

Prepared in conjunction with
The Center for Youth Ministry Development

Catholic Families Series
Growing in Faith: A Catholic Family Sourcebook
© 1990 Salesian Society, Inc. / Don Bosco Multimedia
475 North Ave., Box T, New Rochelle, NY 10802

Library of Congress Cataloging-in-Publication Data
Growing in faith: a Catholic family sourcebook / edited by John Roberto
  p.   cm.   — (Catholic families series)
  "Prepared in conjunction with the Center for Youth Minsitry
  Development" — T.p. verso.
  Includes bibliographical references.
  ISBN 0-89944-155-6 $12.95
  1. Family—Religous life. 2. Catholic Church—Membership.
I. Roberto, John. II. Center for Youth Ministry Development. III. Series
BX2351.G72 1990   90-44357
248.4'82—dc20   CIP

Printed in the United States of America

9/90   9 8 7 6 5 4 3 2 1

Table of Contents

ABOUT THE AUTHORS

Betty Carter, M.S.W. is director of the Family Institute of Westchester. She is co-director of the Women's Project in Family Therapy. In addition to training and supervision, she counsels couples and families, specializing particularly in marital therapy and therapy of remarried families. She regularly lectures and gives workshops in the United States and Europe, and has published numerous articles and book chapters. She is the co-editor with Monica McGoldrick of The *Changing Family Life Cycle.*

Bernard J. Cook, Ph.D. is professor of systematic theology at Holy Cross College in Worcester, MA. He is the author of a dozen books and numberous articlemong his books are *Ministry to Word and Sacrament* and *Sacraments and Sacramentality.* He is a popular conference speaker.

Reynolds R.(Butch) Ekstrom is a staff member at the Center for Youth Ministry Development. He holds an M.A. in Pastoral Studies from Loyola University of the South and has served as Associate Director of Religious Education for the Catholic Archdiocese of New Orleans. He teaches at universities and dioceses across the country through the Center's Certificate in Youth Ministry Studies program. Butch is the editor and primary author of *Access Guides to Youth Ministry: Pop Culture,* and co-editor of *Access Guides to Youth Ministry: Evangelization* and *Good News for Youth.* He has also written articles on the topics of rock music, youth culture, and adolescent faith development.

James Fowler, Ph.D. is Professor of Theology and Human Development and Director of the Center for Faith Development at Emory University in Atlanta. Dr. Fowler is a pioneer in faith development studies, beginning his research in the early 1970's. Among his books are *Stages of Faith; Becoming Adult, Becoming Christian.*

Rabbi Edwin Friedman, DD is the author of *Generation to Generation — Family Process in Church and Synagogue* and numerous articles and chapters on the theory and application of family therapy to a variety of problems. He has been teaching in the field for over two decades. In addition to lecturing widely and to his counseling practice, Rabbi Friedman conducts his own post-graduate training center for clergy and other helping professionals.

James McGinnis, Ph.D. is co-director of the Institute for Peace and Justice and co-coordinator of the National Parenting for Peace and Justice Network. He has authored or co-authored numerous books including *Parenting for Peace and Justice, Helping Families Care, Helping Kids Care,* and *Journey into Compassion — A Spirituality for the Long Haul.* Jim lecturers and gives workshops nationally and internationally.

Kathleen McGinnis is co-director of the Institute for Peace and Justice and co-coordinator of the National Parenting for Peace and Justice Network. She has authored or co-authored numerous books including *Parenting for Peace and Justice*, *Starting Out Right*, and *Helping Families Care*.

Monica McGoldrick, M.S.W. is an Associate Professor and Director of Family Training for the Department of Psychiatry, UMDNJ-Robert Wood Johnson Medical School, and the Continuing Mental Health Center at Piscataway, N.J. She is co-founder of the Family Institute of Westchester. She edited and wrote a number of articles for The Changing Family Life Cycle, and Ethnicity and Family Therapy. She has also written *Women in Families: A Framework for Therapy* and *You Can Go Home Again*, a popular book on family systems.

John Roberto is the co-founder of the Center for Youth Ministry Development. John holds an M.S. in Religious Education from Fordham University. He is the managing editor of Spectrum Resources, a joint publishing project between the Center and Don Bosco Multimedia, producing print and video resources for youth ministry, family ministry, and religious education. John has authored The *Adolescent Catechesis Resource Manual* and "Principles of Youth Ministry," and served as editor for the following *Access Guides to Youth Ministry: Evangelization, Liturgy and Worship*, and *Justice*.

Dolores Waters served as the research coordinator for Phase One of the Catholic Families Project, compiling an extensive annotated bibliography of resources and writing a research report based on the interviews with families conducted by symposium participants. She holds an M.A. in Theological Studies from the Candler School of Theology at Emory University.

ACKNOWLEDGMENTS

"The Family Life Cycle" by Betty Carter M.S.W. and Monica McGoldrick M.S.W. is reprinted courtesy of Allyn and Bacon from *The Changing Family Life Cycle*, edited by B. Carter and M. McGoldrick (1989).

"A Family View of Rites of Passage" by Rabbi Edwin Friedman is reprinted courtesy of Allyn and Bacon from *The Family Life Cycle*, edited by Betty Carter M.S.W. and Monica McGoldrick M.S.W. (1989).

"Basic Christian Understandings" by Bernard Cooke is reprinted courtesy of Pilgrim Press from *Education for Citizenship and Discipleship*, edited by Mary Boys (1989).

"The Social Mission of the Family" by Jim and Kathy McGinnis is reprinted courtesy of Geneva Press (Westminster/John Knox Press) from *Faith and Families*, edited by Lindell Saywers (1986).

PREFACE TO THE CATHOLIC FAMILIES SERIES

Welcome to the *Catholic Families* series! Through a generous grant from a Catholic foundation, the Center for Youth Ministry has been involved in a five-year plan to explore the dynamics of faith maturing and faith sharing in Catholic families and to develop new initiatives for promoting faith maturity in families throughout the entire family life cycle. Don Bosco Multimedia is serving as the publisher for these new initiatives by introducing a new line of important resources for *Catholic families*, themselves, and for *Church leaders* involved in ministry with them throughout the life cycle.

The Catholic Families Project has been guided by the conviction that the family is the primary context for faith growth and faith sharing. The family, and parents in particular, are the key variable in nurturing faith growth and in sharing the Catholic Christian Story/Tradition with children and youth. The Project has been a national effort, involving hundreds of Church leaders in pastoral ministry, family ministry, religious education/catechesis, social ministry, liturgical ministry, youth ministry, young adult ministry, ministry with ethnic cultures, and in the RCIA.

The Catholic Families Project has been conducted in three stages:

Phase One: Research and National Symposium
In the first year the project developed a theoretical-research base for identifying how families grow in faith and the patterns and dynamics of how families share Christian faith. The implications of the research base for strengthening family life and ministerial and educational efforts with families was developed through a national symposium held in August 1988. *Growing in Faith: A Catholic Family Sourcebook* is the sourcebook which provides the foundational principles and theoretical-research understandings from which new initiatives with families were created.

Phase Two: Program Development
Over a two year span, the Center and the participants from the national symposium created and piloted new initiatives, grounded in the theoretical-research base, for promoting faith maturity in families throughout the entire family life cycle. Many of the new initiatives addressed faith maturing and faith sharing throughout the entire family life cycle: *Faith Transmission and Growth in Ethnic Families, Transmission of Faith through Rites of Passage and Rites of Growth and Change, Parenting for Faith Growth, Leadership Training for Church Leaders, and Media and the Family.* Other initiatives addressed specific stages of the life cycle: *Families with Young Adolescents, Families with Older Adolescents, Young Adults and the Family.*

Phase Three: Education, Publications, Networking
The creation of publications for use in families, parishes, schools, and college campuses, and the education of Church leaders to utilize the new initiatives, programs, and resources culminates the Catholic Families Project.

The Center for Youth Ministry Development and Don Bosco Multimedia are proud to make available these new programs and resources to assist Church leaders and families themselves in promoting faith maturing and faith transmission in the family system. These resources fill an important need in the contemporary Church. Included in the Catholic Families product line are the following publications:

Families with Young Adolescents
This five-session educational program, designed to assist leaders in working with families of younger adolescents, addresses:
   (1) The Early Adolescent Family: Who Are We?
   (2) Family Health
   (3) Family Influences
   (4) Family Faith Expression
   (5) Family Decision-Making.

Families and Youth
Using the format of DBM's Access Guide series, this book will include foundational essays and practical strategies in the following areas:
   (1) Faith, Faith Development and Faith Transmission
   (2) Emotional Family Process and Faith Transmission
   (3) Family Personality and Faith Transmission
   (4) Culture and Faith Transmission
   (5) Rites of Passage
   (6) Communicating Relational and Sexual Values
   (7) Communicating Moral Values
   (8) Family Networks.

Families and Young Adults
This four-session program assists young adults, both on and off campus to explore their faith story, their family of origin, and the Catholic faith story. Sessions include:
   (1) Young Adult Faith Development
   (2) Young Adults and Their Family of Origin: Impact on Faith
       Transmission
   (3) The Catholic Faith Story
   (4) Empowering Young Adults to Share Their Own Faith Story.

Rites of Passage and Rites of Growth and Change: A Resource Guide
The Resource Guide assists parish leaders and families to recognize that faith is transmitted by celebrating and ritualizing ordinary life experiences and events. It includes a process and models for developing rituals so that parishes and families can ritualize and celebrate these experiences.

Rites of Passage and Rites of Growth and Change: A Family Ritual Guide
The Ritual Guide helps families find life's deeper meaning through heightened awareness of the major rites of passage and through their

participation in the communal celebration in the parish. It includes practical in-family celebrations.

Parenting for Faith Growth: A Parent Education Program
Written for parents, these six booklets address the practical skills parents need for nurturing faith growth and share faith with their children throughout the life cycle: early childhood, later childhood, younger adolescence, older adolescence, young adult, adult children. A Facilitator's Guide for the program leader contains designs for use with families.

A Partnership between Family and Parish:
A Pastoral Plan for the Transmission of Faith
To assist Church leaders in all ministries clarify the roles, relationships, and responsibilities of the family, parish community and parish ministries in the transmission and nurturing of faith, the Catholic Families Project has created a pastoral plan for faith transmission across the entire family life cycle. This Plan is intended as a guide to foster a collaborative approach among leaders and ministries as they develop programs and materials with a family perspective in the transmission of faith.

Leadership Training Program for Families and Faith
Developed for leaders in all ministries, this program includes complete training designs and handouts on the following topics:
  (1) Family Systems Theory and Family Life Cycle
  (2) Theology of Faith and How Faith is Transmitted
  (3) Impact of Culture upon Family Faith Transmission
  (4) Practical Skills for Using a Family Systems and Life Cycle Perspective.

Media, Faith, and the Family: A Catalog
This media catalog is designed to help both ministers and parents explore the impact of television, movies and other media on family faith and values. This resource helps families to more effectively encounter and interpret media.

Introduction

CATHOLIC FAMILIES SERIES
GROWING IN FAITH:
A CATHOLIC FAMILY SOURCEBOOK

John Roberto

Growing in Faith: A Catholic Family Sourcebook is the sourcebook for the Center for Youth Ministry Development's Catholic Families Project. As a sourcebook it provides the foundational principles and theoretical-research understandings from which new initiatives with families can be created. The Catholic Families Project has been guided by the conviction that the family is the primary context for faith growth and faith sharing. The family, and parents in particular, are the key variable in nurturing faith growth and in sharing the Catholic Christian Story/Tradition with children and youth.

In order to understand the critical role families have in nurturing faith growth and in sharing or transmitting faith, a number of theoretical-research sources were consulted. These sources include family systems theory, family life cycle theory, psychological and developmental research, sociological and cultural research/analysis, and theological reflection on the Catholic Christian faith and Tradition/Story. The exploration of these sources produced a number of important building blocks for developing a family perspective on faith growth and faith transmission. The essays in this book describe these building blocks.

Chapter 1, "Foundational Principles for Faith Growth and Faith Sharing in Families" by John Roberto synthesizes the theoretical-research foundation, presented in this book, into a series of principles that guide the thinking and creation of new initiatives through the Catholic Families Project.

Chapter 2, "The American Family: Change and Diversity" by Reynolds R. Ekstrom presents a succinct look at sociological research on the changes in family life, and on families and faith.

Chapter 3, "The Family Life Cycle" by Betty Carter and Monica McGoldrick describes the six stages and life tasks of the family life. They also present variations in the family life cycle to accommodate the needs of poor families, ethnic families, divorced and remarried families, and immigrant families.

Chapter 4, "A Family View of Rites of Passage" by Rabbi Edwin Friedman presents the tremendous power of rites of passage (or transition) for healing and religious growth in the family. Friedman looks at the potential in the ceremonies surrounding four natural life cycle events: birth, puberty, marriage, and death; as well as around three nodal events: divorce, retirement, and geographical uprooting.

Chapter 5, "Basic Christian Understandings" by Bernard Cooke develops five elements of down-to-earth knowledge people need in order to deal religiously with the experienced reality of their human life: Jesus, Church, salvation, revelation, and the Christian life. These five elements provide a foundation for faith sharing.

Chapter 6, "Faith Development through the Family Life Cycle" by James Fowler creatively correlates his six stages of faith development with family systems theory and the family life cycle. This correlation produces specific directions for nurturing faith maturing in families across the entire life span.

Chapter 7, "The Social Mission of the Family" by Jim and Kathy McGinnis analyzes five forces affecting family life today (materialism, individualism, racism, sexism, violence and militarism) and proposes strategies for helping families assume responsibility for the transformation of the world.

Chapter One

FOUNDATIONAL PRINCIPLES FOR FAITH GROWTH AND FAITH SHARING IN FAMILIES

John Roberto

The Catholic Families Project has been guided by a series of convictions about the importance of the family in nurturing faith, sharing the Catholic Christian Faith Tradition/Story, and living out this faith in the family and world. We believe that it is of highest priority that the family be respectfully understood, critically assessed, and pastorally assisted by the Church today.

We believe that. . .

* the family is a *domestic Church* — a community of life and love in service to God's Kingdom in history — with a specific identity and mission. The family itself is part of the Church.
* the family is the primary context for faith growth and faith sharing. The family, and parents in particular, are the key variable in nurturing faith growth and in sharing the Catholic Christian Story/Tradition with children and youth. Second only to an individual's free response to God, the family profoundly shapes children's and youth's religious identity.
* empowering families to undertake and realize their specific mission is an essential goal of all Church ministries. Faith is nurtured and the Catholic Christian Story/Tradition shared when the family is actively engaged in carrying out its mission.
* we encounter God in the experiences and events of everyday life—in our work, in our relationships, in our family life—and in the Catholic Christian Tradition/Story—in the Scriptures, in prayer, in the sacraments. We believe that family life is a privileged locale for encountering God in everyday life experiences and in the Christian Tradition/Story.
* a family systems perspective provides a way of seeing the dynamics of family life as opportunities for faith to mature and for the Catholic Christian Story to be communicated. Effective family functioning provides a positive and healthy context for faith maturing.
* the family life cycle stages—and their life tasks and transitions—provide opportunities to promote faith growth in the entire family system across generations. The rites of passage that each life cycle change precipitates create opportunities for transformation because the family system unlocks or

is more open to change at these times. The Church's basic sacraments revolve around many of these life cycle changes.

* the parish community and its variety of ministries are to be in *partnership* with the family in nurturing the faith growth of family members, in sharing the Catholic Christian Tradition/Story, and in empowering the family to live the Christian faith in the family and in the world. The parish community is one of the only institutions with families (across the entire life span) as a regular part of its membership.

Our convictions are rooted in a broad *understanding* of the role of the family, drawn from a variety of sources including developmental research, social science research, systems theory, and theological reflection. This essay presents a series of *foundational principles*, developed through the Catholic Families Project, to guide the development of new pastoral and educational approaches that will take seriously the family context for faith maturing, for sharing or transmitting the Catholic Christian Tradition/Story, and for living out this faith in the family and in the world.

CHRISTIAN FAITH

Christian faith is a gift of God whose grace touches the inner core of a person and disposes one toward a lived relationship with God in Jesus Christ.

Christian faith, as a lived reality, has three essential and constitutive dimensions — an activity of trusting, an activity of believing, and activity of doing.

Faith as a *gift* invites a free response to share life in relationship with God who is the very source of life. This response is a personal encounter with God in Christ which transforms a person's way of life. As a response of the whole person, genuine faith involves an affective dimension, the activity of trusting; a cognitive dimension, the activity of believing; and the behavioral dimension, an activity of doing.

As an *activity of trusting*, Christian faith is "an invitation to a relationship of loyalty to and trust in a faithful God who saves through Jesus Christ by the power of the Spirit." (Groome 75) This activity of faith also involves trust in and loyalty to other persons. As an *activity of believing*, Christian faith is a particular way of interpreting our experience in light of the Good News and the continuing tradition of the Church so that it leads to a deeper and expanded understanding of living as a Catholic Christian. This activity of faith necessarily involves the gradual development of deep convictions and a fuller understanding of the doctrinal expression of the Catholic faith. As an *activity of doing*, Christian faith is an active response to the mandate of God's Kingdom — to love God by loving neighbor, especially in the living and pursuit of justice, peace, equality, and so on. This activity of faith calls us to transform the world through "a life of loving service on all levels of human existence — the personal, the interpersonal, and the social/political." (Groome 76)

Christian faith is covenantal. It is trust and loyalty, commitment between persons and within groups that is ratified and deepened by a shared trust in and loyalty to God in Jesus Christ.

Christian faith as *covenantal* is a dynamic pattern of personal trust in and loyalty to:

* God as the source and creator of all value, as disclosed and mediated in Jesus Christ, and through the Church, as inspired by the Holy Spirit. As such Christian faith is *Trinitarian* faith.
* The actual and coming reign of God as the hope and power of the future, and as intending justice and love among humankind. In this sense Christian faith gives us a horizon and vision, a horizon of hope grounded in a trust in the actual, present and coming reign of God.
* God, in Christ, as the Loving, Personal Redeemer and Reconciler calling us to repent and freeing us from the bondage of Sin. Christ frees us from anxiety about death, from the threat of separation from love, and from our hostility and alienation from each other.
* The Church, as Body of Christ, as visible and invisible extension of the ministry and mission of Christ. (Fowler 97)

Growth in Christian faith is a gradual, lifelong, developmental process involving the total person in a continuing journey toward maturity as a Christian.

Lastly, Christian faith is a gradual, lifelong, developmental process involving the total person — head, heart, and lifestyle. Christian faith is a process of conversion, never a point of arrival. The research of James Fowler and others on faith development emphasize this lifelong understanding. Human development, faith development, and the family life cycle are all intertwined as a person grows toward maturity in faith. Commitment to and growth of a mature faith happens over a long period of time.

What are the characteristics of mature Christian faith that we want to promote? Growth toward maturity in faith involves both a life-transforming relationship to a loving God and a consistent devotion to serving others. Mature faith integrates eight core dimensions:

* Trusting in God's saving grace and firmly believing in the humanity and divinity of Jesus Christ.
* Experiencing a sense of personal well-being, security and peace.
* Integrating faith and life — seeing work, family, social relationships, and political choices as part of one's religious life.
* Seeking spiritual growth through study, reflection, prayer, and discussion with others.
* Seeking to be part of a community of believers in which people give witness to their faith and support and nourish one another.
* Holding life-affirming values, including commitment to racial and gender equality, affirmation of cultural and religious diversity, and a personal sense of responsibility for the welfare of others.

* Advocating for social and global change to bring about greater social justice.
* Serving humanity, consistently and passionately, through acts of love and justice. (Benson and Eklin 10)

THE IDENTITY AND MISSION OF THE CATHOLIC FAMILY

*The family is a **domestic church** — a community of life and love in service to God's Kingdom in history — with a specific identity and mission.*

The mission of the family is to become an intimate community of persons; to serve life in its transmission, physically and spiritually; to participate in the development of society; and to share in the life and mission of the Church.

A Family Perspective in Church and Society provides a definition of the family that guides the pastoral and education work of the Catholic Families Project.

> ...the family is an intimate community of persons bound together by blood, marriage, or adoption, for the whole of life. In our Catholic tradition, the family proceeds from marriage — an intimate, exclusive, permanent, and faithful partnership of husband and wife. The definition is intentionally normative and recognizes that the Church's normative approach is not shared by all. (19)

While this definition is restrictive in some senses, it also proposes a broader view in the following ways:
 (a) it includes multiple generations and extended family members
 (b) it recognizes that many persons are involved simultaneously in several families
 (c) it includes single persons since they have families of origin
 (d) it recognizes that there are other covenantal relationships in the family besides marriage (parent-children, siblings
 (e) it recognizes families that are created by adoption.

It is important to note that different ethnic groups define "family" differently from the dominant American definition that has focused on the intact nuclear family. Many ethnic groups view family as the entire extended network of relatives. Other ethnic groups tend to focus on a wide informal network of kin and community in their even broader definition of family. Still other ethnic groups include all their ancestors and all their descendents in their definition of family.

The Church teaches that the family has a unique identity and mission that permeates its tasks and responsibilities. This identity and mission is shaped by a Christian vision of family life.

> This vision is rooted in the covenantal love of Jesus Christ. It holds that the family 'constitutes a special revelation and realization of ecclesial communion, and for this reason too, [the family] can and should be called the domestic church.' (*Familiaris Consortio* 21) This vision proclaims that family life is sacred and that family activities are holy. It also

proposes a unique family mission. It places the family at the service of the building up of God's Kingdom in history. (*Familiaris Consortio* 49) The mission also calls families to protect and reveal their intimate community of life and love. (*Family Perspective* 8)

The family as a *domestic church* means that the family itself is part of the Church. "It has the same functions as the rest of the Church, but it is the Church in a family way. ...Evangelization, catechesis, worship, and ministry will all have their family expressions, but because of the earthly character of family life, they will be rather secular in appearance. ...For it is the life of the family itself which is its basic spiritual resource. And it is the way in which the love of God and neighbor are joined together in the family that give it is most fundamental charge. (Thomas 16-17)

This mission of the family as a *domestic church* — a community of life and love in service to God's Kingdom in history — is realized through four very specific tasks. Empowering families to undertake and realize these tasks is an essential goal of all church ministries.

Task 1: The family is an intimate community of persons.

Task 2: The family serves life in its transmission, both physically by bringing children into the world, and spiritually by handing on values and traditions as well as developing the potential of each member at every age.

Task 3: The family participates in the development of society by becoming a community of social training, hospitality, and political involvement and activity.

Task 4: The family shares in the life and mission of the Church by becoming a believing and evangelizing community, a community in dialogue with God, and a community at the service of humanity. (*Family Perspective* 20-21)

We can also view the mission of the family in relation to God's covenant creativity. Families are an essential part of God's covenant creativity. The three major functions in God's purposes for families are procreation, socialization, and becoming unique individuals before God. (Anderson)

As part of God's co-creation or our co-creation with God, *procreation* is a basic task and calling of family life. Similarly, families contribute to social stability by the process of *socialization*. This means teaching norms, values and rules; forming habits and attitudes in relation to stories and orientations; teaching behaviors and skills, and the like. In the third place, families contribute to the possibility of people *becoming unique individuals before God*. As Johannes Metz would say, our families are the context where we first begin the journey toward becoming "subjects before God" — agents in our own history and responsible selves, as it were. (Fowler 99)

THE FAMILY AS A SYSTEM GROWING OVER TIME

The family is not a collection of individuals, but a living and developing system whose members are essentially interconnected.

The family exhibits great diversity in structure with nuclear, extended, single or multiple generations, two-parent, single-parent, single-earner, dual-earner, childless, blended, and separated families.

Central to the family as the primary context of faith growth and transmission is the concept of the family as a developing system, moving through time.

A systems approach elevates the interaction and cooperation among the members of the whole to a place of prominence and places less emphasis upon the solitary action of the individual. It does not see the whole as merely a collection of individuals, but as a system of relationships, expectations, and responsibilities by which people connect the very heart of who they are to other people. (*Family Perspective* 23)

The family as a system is a new reality. The family systems model shows how each person in a family plays a part in the whole system. John Bradshaw summarizes the concept of a family as a system by using the letters of the word FAMILIES.

F. *Feedback Loops versus Cause/Effect.* The family systems notion sees the family as a dynamic social organism. Such an organism functions by means of interaction and interdependence. Family member behavior is cyclical rather than casual.

A. *Autonomy or Wholeness.* The family is a total organism — the whole is greater than the sum of its parts. Everyone in the family is affected by everyone else. Each individual is partly a whole and wholly a part. A whole new social concept of emotional dis-ease [and health] emerges from this realization. Individuals are not emotionally dis-eased — whole families are.

M. *Marriage as the chief Component.* The marriage is the Chief Component in the family. The health of the marriage determines the health of the family.

I. *Individual Roles.* All families have roles. The role of parent is to model the following: how to be a man or woman; mothering and fathering; how to be a person; how to express feelings and desires; how to be in an intimate relationship; how to be functional human beings; how to have good boundaries. The role of children is to be curious and learn. In healthy families the roles are flexible; in dysfunctional families the roles are inflexible.

L. *Laws or Rules.* All families have laws or rules that govern the system. Laws include issues like household maintenance, body care, celebration, social life, financial issues, privacy and boundaries.

I. *Individuation/Togetherness Tension.* The tension in families results from the individuation/togetherness polarity. The need to be unique and self-actualized often clashes with the need to conform for the sake of the system.

E. *Equilibrium.* Families as social systems operate according to the laws of complementarity. If one parent is angry a lot, the other parent is mild and soft-spoken. Like a mobile, the system will always try to come to rest and balance. Families can be open (always in gentle motion) or closed (frozen or rigid).

S. *Systems Needs.* Like individuals, systems have needs. Families, like all social
systems, have need for productivity (food, clothing and shelter), emotional
maintenance (touching, stroking, warmth); good relationships (love,
intimacy); individuality and difference (a sense of worth and self-
actualization); stimulation (excitement, challenge, fun); unity (a sense of
belonging and togetherness); a sense of unified structure; a sense of
responsibility; a sense of joy and affirmation; and a spiritual grounding.
Parents also play the role of nourishing teachers, giving their children time,
attention and direction. (Bradshaw 39-40)

*The family is a three or four generational system moving through time in a life
cycle of distinct stages with particular tasks to accomplish and challenges to face
in order to prepare itself and its members for further growth and development.*

*The individual life cycle takes place within the family life cycle, which is the
primary context of human and faith development.*

The family life cycle perspective frames problems and strengths within the
course the family has moved along in its past, the tasks it is trying to master, and
the future toward which it is moving. The individual life cycle takes place within
the family life cycle, which is the primary context of human and faith
development. Relationships with parents, siblings and other family members go
through stages as one moves along the life cycle, just as parent-child and spouse
relationships do. The stages of the family life cycle, as described by Carter and
McGoldrick (see Chapter 3), include:

1. Leaving home: single young adults
2. The joining of families through marriage: the new couple
3. Families with young children
4. Families with adolescents
5. Launching children and moving on
6. Families in later life

The family life cycle comprises the entire emotional system of at least three,
and now frequently four, generations. For one thing the three or four different
generations must accommodate to life cycle transitions simultaneously. While one
generation is moving toward older age, the next is contending with the empty nest,
the third with young adulthood, forming careers and intimate peer adult
relationships and having children, and the fourth with being inducted into the
system. For example, the birth in a new generation corresponds with child-bearing
in the parent generation and with grand-parenthood in the eldest generation (See
Chapter 6, Chart 2). If you look at the middle years of childhood, you see a settling
down—roughly the period of the thirties for the parents; then you see grandparents
planning for retirement. In adolescence, you see parents dealing with mid-life
transition—a 40's re-evaluation—and you see grandparents dealing with
retirement. Then, as that child we've been following comes to the level of being an
unattached adult, ready for marriage and courtship, we see parents dealing with

issues of middle-adulthood and with renegotiating their marriage relationship. The grandparents, at this point, begin dealing with dependency and late-adulthood.

We must be aware that the family life cycle paradigm best describes middle-class families. Divorce and remarriage, poverty, and ethnicity provide three important factors which vary the six-stage family life. Carter and McGoldrick conceptualize the need for families in which divorce occurs to go through one or two additional phases of the family life cycle in order to restabilize and go forward developmentally again at a more complex level. They also emphasize that the adaptation of multiproblem poor families to a stark political, social and economic context has produced a family life cycle pattern that varies significantly from the middle-class paradigm so often and so erroneously used to conceptualize their situation. Ethic families negotiate the life cycle tasks in ways that vary from the middle-class presentation. (Carter and McGoldrick)

Family strengths enable families to operate effectively as a system meeting the needs of family members and the family as a whole.

Beginning with family strengths rather than focusing on what is wrong with families is a transformation in the way we think about families. "Family strengths can be defined as those relational patterns, interpersonal skills, attitudes, competencies, values, and individual psychological characteristics that help the family to work." (*Family Perspective* 24) Supporting, enhancing and cultivating the sources of strength in family life, rather than focusing on family problems, positively and significantly affects the quality of family life and the health of family members. This provides a positive and healthy context for faith growth and faith sharing.

The research of Nick Stinnet and John DeFrain, and Dolores Curran have identified traits or qualities of family strengths that can be supported and cultivated. Briefly summarized these traits are. . .

Commitment: an investment of time, energy, spirit, and heart; a strong sense of commitment to stay related during times of transition, difficulty or crisis. Family members are dedicated to promoting each other's welfare and happiness — and they expect the family to endure. They have a sense of shared responsibility for the family.

Time Together: spend both quality and quantity of time together; shares leisure time together. The family has a sense of play and humor.

Appreciation: appreciate and respect, affirm and support each other.

Communication: develop and use skills in communication, negotiating and resolving problems and differences in a positive and constructive way.

Religious and Moral Wellness: possess a solid core of moral and religious beliefs, promoting sharing, love, and compassion for others. The family teaches a sense of right and wrong. They have a strong sense of family in which rituals and traditions abound. They value service to others.

Coping with Crisis: internally drawing on the above strengths, developing adaptability; relying on external resources: social network and community organizations. The family admits to and seeks help with problems. (Stinnet and DeFrain, Curran)

In their book, *Five Cries of Parents*, Merton and Irene Strommen identify five sources of family strength, drawn from research and experience, that can help families grow in faith:

(1) *understanding, affirming parents*

(2) *close, caring families* which exhibit parental harmony, effective parent-child communication, a consistent authoritative/democratic parental discipline, and parental nurturing

(3) *moral, service-oriented beliefs* developed through demonstrative affection, consistent authoritative (democratic) discipline, and inductive discussion

(4) *a personal, liberating faith* which emphasizes God's love and acceptance, establishes and maintains a close relationship to God, and empowers people to reach out and care for others, developed through daily interaction, structured times of worship and works of justice and service as a family

(5) *receiving help* by admitting the needs to draw on the skilled resources of outside experts when problems arise. (Strommen)

THE FAMILY AND ETHNICITY

Ethnicity interacts with the family life cycle at every stage. Families differ in their definition of "family," in their definition of the timing of life cycle phases and the tasks appropriate at each phase, and in their traditions, rituals, and ceremonies to mark life cycle transitions. Ethnicity has an impact on one's outlook on life, expression of faith, and faith traditions.

The adjustment to a new culture by those who immigrate to the United States is a prolonged developmental process that has a profound impact on faith growth through the family life cycle and on faith transmission.

Ethnicity patterns our thinking, feeling, and behavior in both obvious and subtle ways, although generally operating outside of our awareness. It plays a major role in determining what we eat, how we work, how we relate, how we celebrate holidays and rituals, and how we feel about life, death, and illness. Monica McGoldrick describes ethnicity as

> a concept of a group's "peoplehood" based on a combination of race, religion, and cultural history, whether or not members realize their commonalities with each other. It describes a commonality transmitted by the family over generations and reinforced by the surrounding community. But it is more than race, religion, or national and geographic origin, which is not to minimize the significance of race or the special problem of racism. It involves conscious and unconscious processes that fulfill a deep psychological need for identity and historical continuity. It unites those who conceive of themselves as alike by virtue of their common ancestry, real or fictitious, and who are so regarded by others. (Carter and McGoldrick 56-57)

There are at least three distinct modes of negotiating an ethnic cultural experience in the United States today. The development of identity and faith in family members of ethnic cultures depends to a large extent on how the family system and/or their community negotiate their ethnic experience within the broader society.

Mainstream implies the extent to which mainstream goals and values are embraced by an ethnic group (family, community). This group represents families who have embraced the mainstream culture and its ways. For immigrant families this may even mean walling off the past and forcing their children to speak English only and never talking about the country they left behind.

Minority implies the extent to which socialization is promoted in order to cope with one's minority status. Families may wall off the new culture, living and working in an ethnic enclave, never making an effort to learn English or to negotiate the American system. These families may have acquiesced to the negative stereotypical behaviors of minority group status in the United States and become alienated from the mainstream culture and its ways.

Ethnic Cultural or *Bi-cultural* implies the extent to which socialization is influenced by the ethnic cultural context, passing on to their children stories and traditions, while at the same time learning the ways of the new culture. A *bicultural identity* may not be in agreement with all the social dictates of mainstream American life. This group has firmly rejected the roles and values of the minority group, priding itself in the rich heritage of its ethnic experiences and tradition. The mainstream may be valued, but its acceptance is second to providing children and youth with an understanding of their 'roots.'

Ministry with families of ethnic cultures must recognize these three modes or triple consciousness that families experience. It also means recognizing the dual socialization (into the mainstream culture and into an ethnic culture) that so many children and youth of ethnic cultures experience. This dual socialization often creates stress and conflict, especially where there is conflict between the values, images, ideals of the mainstream culture and the ethnic culture, often represented by the parents and extended family. To reconcile into one's identity values and images that are diametrically opposed poses an extraordinary challenge.

Any life cycle transition can trigger ethnic identity conflicts since it puts families more in touch with the roots of their family traditions. How the rituals of transition are celebrated can make an important difference in how well the family will adjust to the changes. (See Friedman's essay in Chapter 4 of this volume.) All situational crises—divorce, illness, job loss, death, retirement—can compound ethnic identity conflicts causing people to lose a sense of who they are.

Migration and the adjustment to a new culture presents families with another set of challenges which have profound impact on faith growth and faith transmission.

McGoldrick notes,

> How immigrants negotiate their new culture in many ways will depend on
> many factors, such as how much time has passed since immigration, their
> life cycle stage at the time of immigration, and the circumstances that led
> them to migrate: did they come alone as young adults, or as young
> children with their nuclear family, or in their later years as part of a mass
> migration because of political or economic oppression? All who migrate
> must deal with conflicting cultural norms of the country of origin and of
> the United States. A person's cultural identity will depend on his or her
> facility with the new language; economic and political situation;
> flexibility in making new connections with work, friends, and
> organizations such as church, schools, government bureaucracies, and the
> health-care system; and remaining connections to the country of origin.
> (Carter and McGoldrick 59)

THE FAMILY AND SOCIETY

*Modern society has created a whole new set of social problems which impact
how families grow in faith through the different phases of the life cycle, how they
share faith, and how they live their faith in the family and world.*

Some of these social problems are *economic*, having to do with how society
organizes resources, some are *political*, having to do with how society organizes
power. Other problems are social, having to do with how society structures
relationships among people, and some are *cultural*, having to do with how society
organizes meaning. The American social structures of economics, politics, social
relationships, and culture have a profound impact on faith growth and faith
transmission in families.

Consider briefly, the changing face of poverty in the United States. These
shocking facts, which run counter to the stereotypes so many hold, describe well
the impact of economic and political forces upon families in the United States.
(*Who are the Poor?*)

The gap between poor and rich Americans is widening. The poorest fifth of all
American families receive only 4.6% of the total national family income; the
richest fifth receive 43.5%. These are both the highest percentages in the 40-odd
years the poverty rate has be measured.

Children constitute the poorest age group in the United States. One in five
children in the U.S. live below the poverty level, which is the highest percentage
among eight industrial nations. This 20 percent figure represents one in seven
whites; one in two African-Americans; and two in three Hispanics. In 1970 fifteen
percent of all children lived in poverty.

*People of color, and especially children of color, bear a disproportionate share of the
poverty burden.* The poverty rate for African-American children (45%) and Hispanic
children (39%) under eighteen years old is three times the rate for all Americans.

Poverty is highest among children in single-parent families (55 percent vs. 12 percent in two-parent families). The increasingly higher rates of poverty among female-headed families has been called the feminization of poverty. Women still only make 65% of what men earn, due to discrimination and to employment in lower paying service sector jobs.

Many poor families do not have health care coverage. Eleven million children have no health insurance.

Many families are the victims of changing economic patterns which have eliminated many jobs and created new jobs which will not support a worker and two dependents, causing a dramatic increase in dual career families and a loss of income for single parent families. This has also increased the need for adequate, affordable child care.

Almost 500,000 children are malnourished in the United States.

James and Kathleen McGinnis examine five social problems which have a tremendous impact on Christian families today: materialism, individualism, racism, sexism, and violence and militarism. (Chapter 7)

Materialism: the tendency in affluent societies for objects to become more important than persons. Objects are personified and persons are commodified. The effects of materialism—this commodification of the person—are particularly devastating on families.

Individualism: a consistent lifting up of self over all other considerations, leading to an emphasis on possessions, the separation of personal freedom from its social context (lack of concern for the common good), emphasis on private ownership which entitles me to use my resources any way I want. Individualism promotes a highly competitive society that affects family life and isolates many families. The more that family members pursue personal goals to the detriment of the common good of family and society, the more it is that fractured and unhappy families seem to increase.

Racism: "Today's racism flourishes in the triumph of private concern over public responsibility, individual success over social commitment, and personal fulfillment over authentic compassion." (*Brothers and Sisters to Us* 6) To see the specific effects of racism on families, consider the following: the high poverty and unemployment rates of people of color; the stereotyping of minority people which leads to a lack of positive self-image and low self-esteem for many minority children; the lack of a quality education for children and youth; and the growing housing crisis that plagues minority families.

Sexism: discrimination based on sex leads to unequal pay for the same jobs and unequal access to more responsible and higher paying jobs which often create serious problems for families where it is a woman's income that supports the family. For minority women there is the double burden of discrimination. The cultural consequences of sexism are demonstrated through stereotypes of what it means to be a "man" and what it means to be a "woman" which limit the emotional, physical, and spiritual development of men and women, boys and girls.

Violence and Militarism: as a means of resolving conflicts, from interpersonal to international conflicts, violence and militarism does not seem to be decreasing. Spouse abuse and child abuse are especially frightening manifestations of the escalating violence in our society today. Militarism affects families economically when monies are appropriated to military expenditures rather than to provide families with adequate food, shelter, medical care, and education.

FAMILIES AS THE PRIMARY CONTEXT FOR FAITH GROWTH

Families, and parents in particular, are the key variable in the nurturing and sharing of faith with children/youth. Second only to an individual's free response to God, the family profoundly shapes children's and youth's religious identity.

*Family meets four basic needs for being and well-being: (1) to **belong** and to experience **being irreplaceable**, (2) to experience **autonomy** and **agency**, (3) to participate in **shared meanings** and **rituals**, and (4) to provide for **bodily well-being** — nurture, wellness, and care.*

James Fowler observes that the family is the context in which we participate in the forming of a first sense of *identity*—who I am, who I can become, what I am worth or not worth. In the family, we have our first and most formative experiences of love relationships and of relationships in which we participate with loyalty and care. In *The Hurried Child*, David Elkind helps us to see that one of the important elements of early socialization for children is learning the *family's covenant system*: what freedoms will be given children and what responsibilities will be expected from them, what achievements are expected and what support can be counted on, what loyalty will be expected or required from family members, and what commitment will be given by those who require it. This is a crucially important part of pre-school socialization. It has to be reworked and renegotiated as we move through each of the stages of the personal and family life-cycle. (Elkind 120) This is what makes families so crucially important for the formation of faith. (Fowler 100)

The family, in its diversity of structures, meets four clusters of needs that are essential for being and well-being.

In our families, we learn to *belong* and to experience *being irreplaceable*. On the little stage of the family, where it is safe, we try our first experiences of *autonomy* and *agency*. These two sets of needs balance each other: Belonging and being separate—being *a part*, and being *apart from*. And then there's our first and most formative experiences of participation in *shared meanings* and *rituals*. Finally, the family provides for *bodily well-being*, for nurture, wellness, and care. It provides opportunities for sexual identification through sustained opportunities to relate to people of the same and opposite sex, and to learn something about the meaning of our gender. (Fowler 100)

Research points to the fact that parents are potentially the greatest influencers of their children's values, religious belief, and behavior. What are some of the reasons parents (and the family system) are so important?

* [Parents have a] closeness to the child (*proximity*) over a long period of time (*longevity*). (Williams)
* The following elements increase the influence of parents (or other significant adults): a) *modeling*: the effect of example has always been understood to be important; b) *agreement*: when parents agree on the importance of religion to them and the messages they convey are consistent, the power of influence increases; c) *congruence*: example is more powerful when parents talk about their actions and when what they say is consistent with what they do. (Williams)
* Parents who talk at home about religious activity and motivation are far more likely to have children who have positive attitudes toward religion. (Williams)
* The influence of congregations, parents, schools, and peers is best exercised in a *warm, supportive environment*. In spite of the superior power of parents to influence, if the family relationship lacks warmth, support, and acceptance, most children and adolescents will seek those qualities elsewhere. (Williams)
* ...we can say that there are four different ways the family of origin affects the religious imagination of one of its offspring: 1) the relationship between the parents of the child . . .; 2) the relationship of the parents to one another; 3) the religious devotion of both parents, especially if they are very devout; 4) the perception by the child of the parent as religiously influential, which presumably indicates the parent's explicit attempt to teach religion. (Greeley 60)

The Church has traditionally taught that parents are the primary educators of their children. This teaching highlights both the rights and the responsibilities of parents. The teaching of Vatican II is a restatement of what has been taught before, and what has been articulated in more recent documents. The Declaration on Christian Education states:

> Parents must be acknowledged as the first and foremost educators of their children. Their role as educators is so decisive that scarcely anything can compensate for their failure in it ...the family is the first school of those social virtues which every society needs. It is particularly in the christian family ...that from their earliest years children should be taught ...to have a knowledge of God, to worship Him, and to love their neighbor. (Paragraph 3)

FAMILY FAITH GROWTH AND TRANSMISSION

Growth in faith through the entire life cycle and the sharing/transmission of the faith story is a complex process involving the family, the community of faith, and the multiple ministries of that community of faith: liturgy and worship, ritual life, religious education/catechesis, and service to the world.

*The parish community and its variety of ministries are to be in **partnership** with the family in nurturing the faith growth of family members, in sharing the Christian Tradition/Story, and in empowering the family to live the Christian faith in the family and in the world.*

No one ministry or institution (family, parish) bears the total responsibility for nurturing faith growth. It is the partnership between family and the parish and its multiple ministries that provide the most effective means for nurturing faith growth. The foundational principles in the preceding sections of this essay have already attested to the formative impact of the family system. In this section, we will examine the connection between a family systems perspective and the multiple ministries of the parish community. We will be looking for the opportunities that this connection offers to all those in pastoral and educational ministry.

It is important to note that faith community's life in general is extremely important for faith maturing. The systems perspective that was used to examine the family can be applied to the parish community as well. Looking at the entire parish system, six aspects of congregational life were identified in a recent study as promoting maturing in faith and stronger congregational and denominational loyalty. They were

(1) formal Christian education programs for adults and children/youth;

(2) quality of Sunday worship;

(3) service to those in need;

(4) personally experiencing the care and concern of other members;

(5) perceiving the congregation to be warm and friendly;

(6) perceiving the congregation to encourage questions, challenge thinking, and expect learning.

The more each aspect is present in the congregation the greater the maturity of faith and the stronger the loyalty of the individual member. An important additional factor is high degrees of faith maturity exhibited by the pastor, educators, and leaders. (Benson et al. 51) Even though we will focus on the ministries of the parish community, it is important to keep in mind the formative aspect of the entire system.

RITUAL AND LITURGY

The rituals and ceremonials of the faith community significantly shape the faith of its members.

Family is the primary force operating in rites of passage. It is really the family that is making the transition to a new stage of life. The whole family goes through the passage at nodal events in the life cycle, and the passage often begins months before and ends months after the ceremony. The entire rite of passage, including the ceremony and the time before and after it, are opportune periods for inducing change in the family system.

The parish community, through its ministry before and after the celebration of rites of passage, has the potential for significantly enhancing the faith of the family and its individual members.

While the process of maturing in faith is complex and diverse, at the heart of faith formation is participation in the Church's rites and sacramental life. John Westerhoff has written, "When we ask, what is most significant in the shaping of *faith...*, *character* (a people's sense of identity and their disposition to behave in particular ways), and *consciousness* (a people's attitudes and awarenesses), the answer is the rituals and ceremonials of a people's primary community. These symbolic actions, words, and behaviors, which express and manifest the community's sacred narrative, significantly influence a people's faith and life." (142) There is tremendous formative influence inherent in ritual ceremonial practices and experiences. In this section we will examine the potential of life cycle celebrations and of ritualizing individual- and family-life experiences and life cycle events.

Edwin Friedman (Chapter 5) has been a pioneer in viewing life-cycle celebrations within a family systems perspective and in unlocking the religious growth and healing potential of rites of passage. He shows how the ceremonies surrounding such nodal occasions in an individual's life may be conceived as family events. "A family approach to life-cycle events also enhances the holiness inherent in the tradition, because religious values are far more likely to be heard when family process is working toward the success of the passage, rather than against it."

Friedman has developed several key insights to guide the way we conceptualize rites of passage in a family systems perspective. On the basis of his experience with families of many cultures, he asserts that these insights (or principles) regarding rites of passage apply for families regardless of cultural background. Here is a brief synthesis of Friedman's insights:

1. The rite of passage is more than the ceremony, and the individuals going through the passage are more than those identified with the ceremony. Ceremonies do focus the events by bringing family processes to the surface through the conscious contact of family members with each other.

2. The rites of passage always indicate significant movement in a family system. Family systems seem to unlock during these periods.

3. Rites of passage are family events that arise at the time they do because of emotional processes that have been at work in the nuclear and extended family of the member(s) who is (are) the focus of the ceremony.

4. The ceremony or the event itself reflects the fact that processes in the family have been undergoing change and are in a state of flux.

5. The ceremony and the time before and after it are therefore opportune periods for inducing change in the family system. The most important time for becoming involved with a family system is in the months before and after the celebration. By getting things going right before any given ceremony, all the natural healing processes that age old traditions have captured in their rites of passage will take over, and at the celebration, do much of the work of healing and religious formation. An awareness of family process can enable a minister to draw on the natural strengths in families to enrich religious experience. By facilitating the meaningful involvement of family members at life cycle ceremonies, ministers are in fact allowing natural healing processes to flow, and doing what religion had always intuited but what modern times has come to be called therapy.

6. There seem to be certain "normal" time periods for the change and working through of emotional processes at times of life cycle transition, and attempts to hasten or shorten those periods unduly are always indications that there are important unresolved issues in the family relationship system. (Friedman)

What are the rites of passage that hold great potential for faith growth and faith transmission? Friedman identifies four natural life cycle events: death, marriage, pubescence, birth; and three nodal events that are more a creation of the times in which we live: divorce, retirement, geographical uprooting. It is important to note that the basic sacraments of the Church revolve around the natural life cycle changes. The Church has ceremonies and ritual for each of these life cycle changes, and church members can provide support to the family at such changes. The parish community, through its ministry before and after the celebration of rites of passage, has the potential for significantly enhancing the faith of the family and its individual members.

Ordinary life experiences have the potential for becoming religiously significant experiences when the sacred is realized, ritualized, and/or celebrated. The family has an important role in ritualizing individual- and family-life experiences and life cycle events.

The parish community, through its rites of celebration, has the potential for enhancing the family's role in ritualizing individual- and family-life experiences and life cycle events.

There are definitive moments within the family system, the lives of individual family members, and the life of the faith community which offer opportunities for celebration and ritualization. To uncover the religious significance of life experiences and events families need to recognize and celebrate life cycle events — major rites of passage (like birth, death) *and* rites of growth and transition (like graduations). The faith community needs to assist families in making the connections between the liturgical year celebrations and sacramental celebrations, and the ordinary activities and life cycle events of families. Understanding the stages of the family life cycle provides families and the faith community with numerous opportunities to ritualize and celebrate transitions. Among the myriad number of opportunities to ritualize family events and transitions are the following: welcoming new members (new baby, re-marriage, adoption), leave taking (divorce, leaving home, loss of relatives or friends), reconciling, welcoming home, sending forth, playing, times of crises (injury, sickness, unemployment), firsts (driver's licence, starting school), seasons of the year, serving others, and accomplishments.

RELIGIOUS EDUCATION/CATECHESIS

*Family religiousness and the amount of exposure to religious
education/catechesis are the two experiences most associated with higher faith
maturity in children and youth. Families and religious education/catechesis are the
critical contexts for the nurturing faith maturity with children and youth.*

The importance of the parish's religious education/catechetical efforts is crucial
for the maturing in faith of its members. One study by the Search Institute
concluded that the two experiences most associated with higher faith maturity in
children and youth are the level of *family religiousness* and the *amount of exposure
to Christian education*; for adults the two experiences were church involvement
and the *amount of exposure to Christian education*. The study also concluded that
the congregational factor most associated with helping people grow in faith is the
degree of effectiveness in Christian education programming. (Benson and Eklin)

Effective education requires particular kinds of process, content, leadership, and
administrative foundations. Effective religious/education not only teaches insight and
knowledge (educational content), but also allows insight to emerge from the crucible of
experience (educational process). "Both ways of learning are powerful, and the two
combinations produce stronger growth in faith than either one alone." (Benson and Eklin)

*A primary task of religious education/catechesis in a family systems perspective
is to provide ways for families to interpret their life experience in ways that lead
them into deeper discipleship.*

We Christians believe that we have been given a language that does in fact help
us to make sense of the world, of a large, broad comprehensive world with its
fundamental issues of good and evil, of promise and limitation, of living and
dying, of suffering and joy, of destruction and creation. We believe that the
language of faith — that is, the stories of the people of Israel; the life, death, and
resurrection of Jesus; the Church and the saints through history, the sacramental
life of the Church — provide for us a pattern of interpretation that gives sense to
our experience and draws us into daily experience in ways that really give us
identity. Because we believe this, we want others to see the world through this lens
and partake in the patterns of interpretation and relationship that the Christian
language enables. We believe that if people hear and learn and use this language,
they will find their most fundamental needs met. (Dykstra)

The educational challenge is to assist families to interpret their everyday life
experiences and events in light of the Christian Tradition/Story and to empower
families to see family life as a privileged locale for encountering God in everyday
life experiences *and* in the Christian Tradition/Story. We need to develop a pattern
of interpretation that is

(1) grounded in religious language and history
(2) provides a constructive vision of the world and personal and social life
(3) calls forth the allegiance of family members because it helps them to
     understand their own experiences and live more fruitful lives
(4) does not take on authoritarian and fundamentalist characteristics. (Dykstra)

The educational/catechetical task is to develop a religious pattern of interpretation that is biblical, grounded in the continuing tradition of the Church, and illuminates the contemporary human experience. Furthermore, our task is to help families and family members experiment with this pattern of interpretation, understand it, and increasingly adopt it as their own in the context of a community of interpretation that does the same with them. (Dykstra)

Faith growth and transmission is enhanced when the religious education/catechetical effort is in partnership with the family through initiatives like family-centered catechesis, adult education, family participation in sacramental catechesis, parent education programs, and parent involvement in program decisions and planning.

There are numerous ways to design religious education/catechetical programming with a family systems perspective. Each of these efforts is aimed at supporting the family as family and explicitly involving or referencing the family as the main context of the process. Research affirms the importance of partnership efforts between the parish's religious education/catechetical programs and family life.

Family factors are also important, particularly in the high school years. Students whose parents are involved in their parish religious education program and students who experience engagement with faith issues as part of family life are more likely than other students to report favorable outcomes (on tests of religious behavior, beliefs, values, and influences). This is an important finding which affirms that families and church-based programs constitute an important partnership. The suggestion here is that programs best affect students when the family is considered part of the religious education team. ...The family that practices faith models a mature faith, and the message does not escape our children. (Kelly, Benson, Donahue 45)

ADULT EDUCATION/PARENT EDUCATION

Research also demonstrates that adult education is critically important to promoting faith growth and faith sharing in families because it nurtures in fathers and mothers a faith that is continually being examined, challenged, and lived more fully. This is the faith that parents share naturally in the flow of family life. Of special importance is adult education which equips mothers and fathers to play a more active role in the religious education of their children, by means of conversation, family devotions, and family helping projects. This requires special efforts to strengthen the spiritual life of parents.

FAMILY RELIGIOUS EDUCATION/CATECHESIS

Family religious education/catechetical programming is an intergenerational involvement of multiple family members, if not the entire family, in the catechetical process. "Family catechesis is the pastoral process which affirms and formalizes the lifelong nurturing process learned and experienced within the family dynamic as the family interacts with the Gospel, the local church, and the world. ...Family catechesis is a catalyst, a resource, a formalizing process that facilitates faith formation as experienced in the personal relationships within the family (spousal, parental, sibling) and in the call within the very fiber of family life to participate in the development of society." (Iannone and Iannone 129-130)

> Family catechesis must deal with the stuff of family life in the way that the family lives, breathes and has its being. Therefore, parish catechetical structures should appreciate and support the everyday ministry of the family as family members relate to other persons, their neighbors, their work, etc. ...Families must trust and act out the conviction that all dimensions of family life are graced, that the Spirit bursts through all impassess, including sin and death, and that Jesus Christ is the Savior for all members of the family at all stages in the human drama. (Iannone and Iannone 131)

> Family catechesis is about the nurturing and maturing in faith that happens formally and informally within a family system at every stage of life. Family catechesis considers both the individual and the family group itself. ...It recognizes that family members have needs and gifts. Catechesis takes place in meeting needs and drawing upon gifts of all family members. Family catechesis deals with the conversion process which happens as family members live together in community and move through the family life cycle. The ministry of catechesis can bring light as well as the challenge of the Gospel to the work of the family agenda. The family agenda can illumine the significance of the Gospel message in different ways through the various stages of the family life cycle. (Purcell and Weithman 11)

From these two descriptions of family religious education/catechesis it is easy to see how this approach fully implements a family systems perspective and the foundational principles outlined in this essay. Family religious education/catechesis has several identifying characteristics:

1. *missionary* — the family as domestic church is called beyond itself to prayer, worship, and service
2. *focused on adults* — adults have the ability to respond fully to God's word. Therefore, family catechesis focuses on adults, and considers both their relationships as adults and their special role as parent.
3. *life-long* — relationships in a family are life-long; thus the need for ongoing catechesis that deals with conversion and reconciliation as relationships change and develop throughout the life cycle.
4. *formal and informal* — sometimes catechesis is explicit and intentional in nature (formal), yet the atmosphere of faith which permeates the home and is the basis for chosen decisions, actions, and relationships can also be a means of catechesis (informal). Informal catechesis also contributes to the continual faith development of the individual and of the family. (Purcell and Weithman 19)

FAMILY PARTICIPATION IN SACRAMENTAL CATECHESIS

Family involvement in the preparation for and celebration of sacraments is essential throughout the life cycle. Sacraments are individual, family, and community events. Edwin Friedman's analysis of rites of passage and family process provides ample reasons for family involvement. Catechesis for the celebration of sacraments involves in an integral way the family, the worshipping community, and the systematic catechetical program. Clarifying these interrelationships and responsibilities is essential to developing a healthy partnership. (DeBoy et al.)

The family has an essential role in the preparation for and celebration of sacraments through the family's lived experience of the sacraments in the family and in the parish community, by becoming more aware of the meaning of a particular sacrament and by sharing this with the family member preparing for the sacrament, by praying together, by being integrally involved in the celebration, by celebrating rituals in the home, and by being actively involved in the parish community and in service to others. (DeBoy et al.)

SOCIAL INVOLVEMENT

Catholic Christian Families realize their identity and mission when they participate as a family and with other families in the transformation of the world.

Realizing peace and justice in the family means addressing peace and justice at all levels of community—the home, the neighborhood, and the global community.

The involvement of the family in the work of justice and service engages the family in fulfilling its mission to "participate in the development of society by becoming a community of social training, hospitality, and political involvement and activity," and " to share in the life and mission of the Church by becoming ...a community at the service of humanity. (*Family Perspective* 20-21) It is clear from Church teaching that families have a definite responsibility to address the pressing social problems that cause injustice, threaten human life and dignity, and undermine family life itself. In order to fulfill its mission families cannot only care for the victims of injustice—the corporal works of mercy. It is also necessary to work to change the situations and structures (economic, political, social, cultural) that create the victims in the first place—the works of justice. Families are called to participate in this world-transforming task.

The family's participation in the Church's social mission helps to realize a number of very important family values (see family strengths description). In addition to service to others, the McGinnises identify the following:

* The "togetherness" set of values is furthered by living the alternative to violence, especially the communication and conflict resolution skills and the family meeting; by simplicity/stewardship, involving sharing of talents and alternative celebrations that focus on people rather than things; and by the family's developing a sense of common mission and one they experience with other families.

* The affirmation and mutual support values are promoted by the centrality of peacemaking in the home itself—living the alternative to violence. Challenging sex-role stereotypes and racial stereotypes affirms and promotes the full human development of each family member. Working with other families, encouraging risk-taking, and supporting one another in actions of all kinds also promote these family values.

* Family members' sense of responsibility and sense of right and wrong are furthered by shared decision-making through the family and the implementation of such decisions. Stewardship—caring for the earth and for future generations as well as sharing talents with family members and others—nurture a deep sense of responsibility. Discussing social problems, encouraging one another to form opinions and stand up for what each believes—all promote these family values.

* The family value of concern for God, the gospel, and prayer is central to the Christian vision of family life. It is Jesus who calls family members to participate in actions that build up the whole body of Christ. It is the resurrection of Jesus that gives family members the hope that if they die to themselves in embracing one another for life and embracing a suffering world, their seeds will bear much fruit. It is the spirit of Jesus—encountered in contemplation, action, and in coming together prayerfully with others—that inspires and gives family members the courage to take the risks necessary to build shalom/family/community—the family community, the neighborhood community, and the global community. (McGinnis and McGinnis)

CONCLUSION

These are the key principles that are guiding the development of new pastoral and educational approaches that will take seriously the family context for faith maturing, for sharing/transmitting the Catholic Christian Tradition/Story, and for living out this faith in the family and in the world. The following essays in this book develop more fully the foundational understandings outlined in these principles. These principles should not be seen as a last word, but rather as guiding understandings for the creation of new initiatives with families.

WORKS CITED

Anderson, Herbert. *The Family and Pastoral Care.* Philadelphia: Fortress, 1984.

Benson, Peter, et al. *Effective Christian Education: A National Study of Protestant Congregations.* Minneapolis: Search Institute, 1990.

Benson, Peter, and Carolyn Eklin. *Effective Christian Education: A National Study of Protestant Congregations — A Summary Report on Faith, Loyalty, and Congregational Life.* Minneapolis: Search Institute, 1990.

Bradshaw, John. *Bradshaw on the Family.* Deerfield: Health Communications, 1988.

Carter, Betty and Monica McGoldrick. "The Family Life Cycle." *Growing in*

Faith.: A Catholic Family Sourcebook Ed. John Roberto. New Rochelle: Don Bosco, 1990.

Curran, Dolores. *Traits of the Healthy Family.* San Francisco: Harper, 1983.

DeBoy, James, et al. *Partners in Catechesis — Family and Catechists.* Dubuque: Brown, 1984.

Dykstra, Craig. "Agenda for Youth Ministry: Problems, Questions, and Strategies." *Readings and Resources in Youth Ministry.* Ed. Michael Warren. Winona, MN: St. Mary's, 1987.

Elkind, David. *The Hurried Child.* Reading, MA: Addison-Wesley, 1981.

Fowler, James. "Faith Development through the Family Life Cycle." *Growing in Faith.: A Catholic Family Sourcebook.* Ed. John Roberto. New Rochelle: Don Bosco, 1990.

Friedman, Edwin. "A Family View of Rites of Passage." *Growing in Faith.: A Catholic Family Sourcebook.* Ed. John Roberto. New Rochelle: Don Bosco, 1990.

Greely, Andrew. *The Religious Imagination.* New York: Sadlier, 1981.

Groome, Thomas. *Christian Religious Education.* San Francisco: Harper, 1981.

Harrington, Michael. *Who Are the Poor?* Washington, DC: Justice for All, 1987.

Iannone, Joseph and Mercedes. "The Educational Ministry of the Christian Family." *Living Light* 21.2 (January 1985).

Kelly, Frank, et al. *Toward Effective Parish Religious Education for Children and Young People.* Washington, DC: NCEA, 1986.

McGinnis, James and Kathleen. "The Social Mission of the Family." *Growing in Faith.: A Catholic Family Sourcebook.* Ed. John Roberto. New Rochelle: Don Bosco, 1990.

NCCB. *A Family Perspective in Church and Society.* Washington, DC: USCC, 1988.

Purcell, Antionette, and Martin Weithman. *Developing a Parish Plan for Family Catechesis.* Washington, DC: NCCD, 1989.

Stinnett, Nick and John DeFrain. *Secrets of Strong Families.* Boston: Little, Brown, 1985.

Strommen, Merton and Irene. *Five Cries of Parents.* San Francisco: Harper, 1985.

Thomas, David. "Home Fires: Theological Reflections." *The Changing Family.* Ed Saxton et al. Chicago: Loyola UP, 1984.

Westerhoff, John. "Catechetics and Liturgics." *PACE* 19 (February 1990).

Williams, Dorothy. "Religion in Adolescence: Dying, Dormant, or Developing. " *SOURCE* 5.4 (December 1989)

Chapter Two

THE AMERICAN FAMILY: CHANGE AND DIVERSITY

Reynolds R. Ekstrom

Contemporary cultural creeds on individualism, self-reliance, and pursuit of the good life make the survival of the American family all the more amazing. At the heart of family life lies love and loving relationships, bonds which unite family members. At its best family stands for interdependence and thorough acceptance. In fact though, the traditional family represents "a historically older form of life." (Bellah 87) Love and marriage in the United States, historically, has fulfilled social functions. They have provided individuals with committed, stable relationships and have served to connect them with the wider world and society. But there are tensions today. Spontaneous intimacy and the short-term are idealized. The longing to "find myself" leads many on quests for personal development and self-fulfillment. Quests for self-knowledge should lead one toward caring relationships with others. Yet should spontaneous, personalized happiness and sudden intimacy become one's goals, formal family role expectations and family obligations "may be viewed negatively, as likely to inhibit such intimacy." (Bellah 85; Veroff 140)

Can we even suppose that we can predict with any confidence, what will happen to the family and family demographics in the years ahead? Some specialists on family life believe that the various changes and tensions experienced, recently, will moderate. Yet few envision a "substantial reversal of trends" in present family patterns.

> ...Concerned groups are taking such steps as helping move remarriage and stepfamilies away from the category "incomplete institutions." As more marriages become voluntary and tentative, so also will divorce and remarriage become behavior that is taken for granted when it occurs. But the preferred goal of most young adults will likely continue to be a permanent first marriage. (Glick 872)

The American family on the whole remains resilient, despite mounting vestiges of personal and interpersonal stresses. Shifts in family patterns — increased divorce, remarriage, cohabitation, lone living, single-parenting — have not been "distributed equally among the affected. Many of those involved are more resilient than others during changes..." Some accept the stresses of uneasy marital or family situations in stride. Others seem able to withstand other social pressures quite effectively. (Glick 871)

Changing and diverse are hallmark terms used to describe families today. The characteristics of the contemporary family make the brief comments in a 1909 speech by William Graham Sumner, outgoing president of the American Sociological Society, quite ironic.

> It appears that the family now depends chiefly on virtue, good sense, conception of duty, and spirit of sacrifice of the parents. They have constantly new problems to meet. They want to do what is right and best. They do not fear change and do not shrink from it. So long as their own character is not corrupted it does not appear that there is any cause for alarm.

Society presents the contemporary family with unanticipated pressures and notable opportunities. The family in the United States now "stands at a crossroads, and confronts fundamental challenges." (*Family Perspective* 4)

Research indicates Americans believe strongly in family life. Family needs and concerns are discussed actively by policy- and law-makers.

> From the time of the American Revolution, the story of the American family is characterized by persistent change, but we know that many of these changes have accelerated over the past generation. Since the Revolution, families in America have lived through the most intense and compacted period of social change in the history of civilization. As we (have) moved from an agricultural to an industrial to a technological society, families have adjusted; experts agree that families are here to stay. (*Family Perspective* 4)

American lifestyles often produce the language and practice of individualism. People easily "develop loyalties to others in the context of families, small communities, religious congregations, and ...lifestyle enclaves." (Bellah 250) As institutions, family life and marriage today are more fragile, more vulnerable, more difficult to maintain. In a sense they have become optional, matters of choice. In recent decades in the USA we have become increasingly tolerant "of people who reject marriage as a way of life." (Veroff 147) A new sense of marriage and new meanings to family life have begun to emerge.

> In this more tolerant atmosphere, alternate forms of committed relationship long denied any legitimacy, such as those between persons of the same sex, are becoming widely accepted. (Bellah 110)

Those new developments can create open, intense, sensitive, and loving relationships. Paradoxically, social conditions can render those relationships vulnerable or fragile too.

There is no longer the "typical" family in the United States. The Church has begun to recognize and name this, seeing changes and diversities in families.

> Each family is unique...(and) families in the United States differ greatly in their structure; in their special needs; in how they are affected by social

trends; in their socioeconomic status; and in their cultural, ethnic, and religious heritages.

Families come in many forms and configurations today: nuclear, extended, single or multiple generations, two-parent, single-parent, single-earner, dual-earner, childless, blended, and separated families. (*Family Perspective* 28)

The American Catholic family, reflecting conditions among U.S. families in general, is undergoing dramatic transition. (Greeley, Religious Imagination 195-97) The percentage of Catholics who are married has dropped since 1976. One-fourth of Catholic teenagers say their natural parents are divorced (this is the same rate as found in the general population). The number of U.S. Catholics separated or divorced doubled (from 5% to 10%) from 1976 to 1985. Historically favoring larger families, the Catholic ideal or preferred family size now mirrors the size favored by mainline American Protestants. Catholics in the USA have blended into the cultural mainstream. (Gallup and Castelli, *American Catholic People* 6)

According to Paul C. Glick, recent research has shed more light on the contemporary complexities of household and family patterns whether Catholic or otherwise. The term household can be used in a narrow way to connote non-family households: people who live alone or with unrelated others. (Waldrop 22) Household thus is distinguishable from family in this sense, a family is a "kinship system of two or more persons which involves commitment to one another...":

Kinship is achieved by marriage, birth, or adoption. Because family structure is linked to family purpose, it is necessary that the family to be defined in such a way that its purposes of procreation, social stability, and individuation might be fulfilled. (Anderson 73)

Demographers will, on the other hand, also utilize the term household, giving it a broader meaning: for example, the sum of U.S. households will be said to include families, lone-living persons, plus those living together who are not kin to each other (like the "lifestyle enclaves" Bellah has referred to). There were 91 million households in America in 1988, broadly speaking (according to the U.S. Census Bureau). Marital couples-with-children accounted for only 27% of all households. Families of some sort accounted for about 70% of all households.

The complexities of social change and life-together have reduced the family's and the household's ability to "tie individuals securely into a sustaining social order." (Bellah 110) Our cultural individualism urges people to take personal responsibility for finding what they want, and for finding relationships (temporary or lasting) that will meet their needs. It is difficult for parents to honestly say that members of their families always do thus and so. We now have many options to pursue and our varied lifestyles can and will reflect individual preferences, or dissimilarities. (Glick 871)

Some observers keenly point out that the family today is "no longer an integral part of a larger moral ecology tying the individual to community, church, and nation." (Bellah 112) In fact, research into changing patterns in our populace tells

us that families and households created during the years 1985-2000 may not much
resemble American households of yesterday. (Exter 46) This should be an issue to
which family specialists, family ministers, family therapists, and all those concerned about faith-transmission in the family life-cycle should particularly attend
with vigor. Desires for self-fulfillment, selfish ego-stroking, sudden intimacy, consumerism, commercialism, suspicions and wariness toward others, and escalating
needs for personal support, in a harried social environment, are having a reverber-
ating impact on the individual and the family in America. Those concerned about
the state of the American family, especially how the family transmits faith and values, must further examine and address the moral ecology issue: the reintegration of
individual, family, wider community, church, and nation.

> The family (today) is the core of the private sphere, whose aim is not to
> link individuals to the public world but to avoid it as far as possible. In
> our commercial culture, consumerism, with its temptations and televi-
> sions, augments that tendency. Americans ...limit of their serious altruism
> is the family circle. Thus the tendency of our individualism to dispose
> "each citizen to isolate himself from the mass of his fellows and withdraw
> into the circle of family and friends," that so worried Tocqueville, indeed
> seems to be coming true. "Taking care of one's own" is an admirable
> motive. But when it combines with suspicion of, and withdrawal from, the
> public world, it is one of the conditions of the despotism Tocqueville
> feared. (Bellah 112)

We might recall the 1950s as a decade of family and tradition. The 1960s? A
time for youthful rebellion and social upheaval. The 1970s? A decade of rootless-
ness and birth of the "me-first" generations. The 1980s were often described as a
period in which many put down some roots and rediscovered some traditional values. What do we make of this in the 1990s? Many current demographic trends
"belie a return to the traditions of the 1950s. The most recent decade is better characterized, overall, as a time of diversity.

Current family patterns reflect this. Our traditions in America and within our
American families are still changing. (Russel and Exter 22) Solutions to problems
today can't be found in 1950s social fashions. The warning signals about recent
stresses on individuals and the moral-ecology shift toward imploding family styles
and sentiments identified by Bellah and others present us 1990s-style challenges
and opportunities. Will we effectively hand on social and religious values? Will we
uncover ways to effectively help ourselves, and others, create lifetimes full of
meaning and commitment and a more socially just society?

"Each decade shapes the next," say Russel and Exter. "And there is never any
going back." (Russell and Exter 22) In transition and resilient, families and households in the 1990s with or without the assistance of family-help agencies and family ministries will struggle with key concerns: crystallization of a new vision of
"family" and its purposes; how to cope and grow as a family/community system;
and how to fulfill personal and family responsibilities in partnership with, not in
withdrawal from, society. (*Family Perspective* 28)

THE AMERICAN HOUSEHOLD:
PAST, PRESENT, AND FUTURE

A significant, long-term development observed in modern societies is "a ubiqui-tous decline in the average size of households." (Santi 833) In the United States in the early 1970s there was a general decrease in the size of family households. The later 1970s brought a substantial decrease in married couple households. A more gentle rate of decline in household size overall in 1980s America represented a continuation of these trends. Divorce, delays of first marriages, and individuals' desires to live alone figured in strongly. Actually the changing living arrangements of adults now seem to exert a central, ever-increasing impact on the average size of American households. (Santi 833, 837)

The U.S. Census Bureau has offered some "best guess projections" about American households, for the period 1985-2000 A.D. Using the term household, the Bureau says 2.69 people lived in the typical American household in 1985. That should shrink to about 2.48 people by the year 2000. One-third of the U.S. popula-tion between 1985-2000 will be baby-boomers (in their 30s and 40s). Their lifestyles and preferences will imbue household trends. (Exter 46) For example, ages for first marriage and rates of divorce will likely rise but slowly.

There were about 91 million American households in 1988 (again, using the term household in its broader sense) according to the Census Bureau. The composition of American households is truly shifting, though, as more and more Americans turn away from the nuclear-family tradition. The number of households headed by indi-viduals aged 35-44 grew by 38% between 1980 and 1988. The so-called "middle-aging of the baby boom" makes this our quickest growing household population seg-ment. Families headed by women, aged 35-44, increased in 1980-88 by 44% to 2.8 million households. Households headed by those 75 or older rose by 25% during the 1980s, but those headed by people 25 or younger fell by 20% during 1980-1988. (Waldrop 22-24) The older householders look to longer life expectancies, improved health care, and other services as particular influences on their lives.

Interestingly, by 1988 over half (57%) of household heads 75 or older lived in "non-family" households. Most lived alone. (Waldrop 27) The median income of all American households in 1987 was $25,986. But with changing household styles in the 1980s, incomes among household types diverged significantly. Some kept up, meeting the challenges of inflation. While others fell behind or tumbled into poverty as we will note again later.

By 2000 the Census Bureau projects 106 million American households, 15 mil-lion more than in 1988, 19 million more than in 1985. The look and lifestyles of many 1990s households should be even less traditional than today. (Exter 45) "The pundits may be saying Americans are returning to traditional life-styles," cautions the journal, *American Demographics*. "But the numbers show that it just isn't so." (Waldrop 22) By 2000, families will number 2 out of 3 American households down from 75% in 1985. Married couples (with children or childless) will be the basis for only about 50% of households down from 58% in the mid-1980s. (Exter 45)

With the middle-aging of the baby boom, the "middle-aging of households" must also come. Householders aged 35-54 will account for the majority of household growth during the 1990s according to the Census Bureau. In the 1990s, though, households headed by 25-34 year-olds will diminish in number noticeably. The baby-bust generation will be aging into its later 20s and early 30s. The actual number of householders aged 55-64 and 65-74 will remain quite stable until 1995. However, households headed by those 75 or older will actually jump to about 11 million by 2000 A.D. (an astonishing 52% increase over the number of these in 1985). (Exter 46-47)

In 1985, there were about 10 million American families headed by women of various ages. About 60% of these families included children. By 2000, there should be close to 13 million families led by women! Non-family households will likely number 34 million by the year 2000. Consider the remarkable differences. In 1940 only 7% of all households were situations in which "one person (was) living entirely apart from relatives or non-relatives." (Glick 867) These rose to 13% in 1960 to 23% in 1980 and to 24% in 1986. By 2000 the Census Bureau estimates that 34 of 106 million households overall or 32% will find inhabitants living alone or with non-family members.

In 1985, 42% of all families were two-earner units. About 15% of families had no earners. (This statistic encompasses retirees and those unemployed.) The median income of the two wage-earner family proved to be 56% greater than the median for single-earner families. (Russell and Exter 28) In the mid-1980s one-fifth of all American households had annual incomes below $10,000. Two-fifths were below $20,000 and three-fifths (or 60%) had incomes of $30,000 or less. Only 11% managed to earn $50,000 or more annually.

As researchers note many households find themselves on the lower end of the income scale. (Russell and Exter 27-28) This is true, in particular, for the fastest-growing among household types — families headed by women and those who live alone.

Householders under 25 years, African-Americans, and Hispanics did not do well with the income distribution in America in the 1980s. In the mid-1980s the median income for African-American households was only 57% of the white household median. Hispanic households accrued 76% of the white median annually. Much of this can be attributed to the growing number of African-American and Hispanic households headed by low income-earning women. (Russell and Exter 26) Economic expansion in the United States during the 1980s has not helped the poor. As economist Robert Samuelson notes, "Economic growth, powerful as it is, won't cure everything. It won't turn low-skilled workers into engineers or technicians ...mend broken families or eradicate crime."

In their book, *Megatrends 2000*, the authors conclude that the American Dream is passing by a large segment of the American population. (Naisbitt and Aburdene 46) A growing awareness recognizes that the root of poverty is failure to create and sustain families.

More than one-third of the 10.4 million families are poor. When couples marry, they overwhelmingly tend to escape poverty; about 94% of mar-

ried couples are not poor. In the early seventies 1 family in 9 was headed
by a women, but beginning in the early 1980s, there were huge increases
in the number of unwed mothers. Today 1 family in 6 is headed by a single mother. There are 5.5 million poor families with children, contrasted
with 4.1 million in 1979. That means the poor are overwhelmingly children. (Naisbitt and Aburdene 46)

As we have noted, it is impossible to fully and accurately predict all the changes
in demographics among American households which will take hold in this decade.
Yet, the dramatic shifting of family patterns and practices should moderate a bit.
The costs and benefits from recent changes in personal and family behaviors, as
Glick observes, have not been distributed equally among those affected. (Glick
871, 876) The statistics we can cite and the comments of specialists only further
underscore the decade of transition and diversity label given to the 1980s, and
intensify our longings to help members of families and households better prepare
to face the challenges and the unknowns that lie ahead.

THE AMERICAN CATHOLIC FAMILY: RELIGION AND SPIRITUALITY

Family researchers indicate that numerous contemporary families seem to cope
and to grow, even with modern life's many surprises, stresses, ups, and downs.
Such families show evidence of a spiritual strength, a wellspring of trust "an
unseen power that can change lives, can give strength to endure the darkest times,
can provide hope and purpose." (Stinnett and DeFrain 100) Researchers character-
ize this spiritual reservoir as one of the most crucial elements to well-being and
harmony in families today. Some families express their family spirituality, currently, through membership in a local church or synagogue. Others tend to make it
manifest through consistent moral behavior, in addressing significant causes and
issues, or through acts of charity and mercy toward others.

How should we speak about an American family spirituality? Some family
members describe it as:

> ...faith in God, faith in humanity, ethical behavior, unity with all living
> things, concern for others or religion. Our definition must be broad
> because strong families are very diverse; their backgrounds differ; their
> experiences are not the same. And because religion is a very touchy sub-
> ject for many people. (Stinnett and DeFrain 101)

Spiritual well-being in families can be imaged as a force that unifies, as caring
individuals who promote love and compassion for others, or a power which helps
one transcend self for the good of something greater. (Brigman 3-9) But what
about family and organized religion in the United States? In the 1830s, Tocqueville
saw organized religion, mainly, as purifying, controlling, and restraining the
"excessive and exclusive taste for (materialistic) well-being" among Americans.
Like the institution we call family, though, religion in American life (still, largely a

privatized phenomenon, i.e., segmented from our political and secular circles) has often provided merely a "haven in a heartless world," loving fellowship and support to individuals, which remains unable, nevertheless, to effectively "challenge the dominance of utilitarian values in the society at large." (Bellah 224)

Not surprisingly, many Americans see religion as an individualistic thing than a larger organizational commitment. If any organizational loyalty is involved, the foremost setting still remains the local congregation. Even though local church is important to many, local church is not usually equated with religion. Religion is seen by many Americans as going beyond transcending, boundaries of local congregation or the individual. Religion is a topic readily handed over to specialists who claim to understand it. A Gallup poll in 1978 found that 4 of 5 Americans believed that each "individual should arrive at his or her own religious beliefs independent of any churches or synagogues." (Hoge 167 and Bellah 226)

> Larger loyalties are not missing but a recent study (also) indicates that even American Catholics, for whom church necessarily has a larger meaning, identify their faith primarily with what goes on in the family and local parish and are much less influenced religiously by the pronouncements of the bishops or even the teachings of the pope than by family members and the local priest. (Fee 229-30 and Bellah 226)

The spiritual resources provided to contemporary families in close relationships, and by supportive, local church contexts make life in general more bearable, less alienating, more conducive to optimism and hope. (Stinnett and DeFrain 119) A recent survey of 80,000 readers of *Better Homes and Gardens* on family spirituality in America revealed the following data (Greer 16-19):

> Do you think spirituality is gaining or losing influence on family life in America?
> Gaining...50%
> Staying the same 14%
> Losing...33%
>
> What do you most want from a religious organization?
> Spiritual development 80%
> A loving, caring group of friends...65%
> A path to salvation 46%
> Self and/or societal improvement.......................................35%
> A sense of serenity 30%
> Ceremonial support (for baptism, weddings, etc.) 27%
> Intellectual stimulation...27%
> Meaning and/or comfort of ritual 14%
> Do not belong to a religious organization 8%
>
> Which activities are most important in your family's spiritual development?
> Following moral principles 73%

Attending religious services 70%

Being members of a church or temple 58%
Reading scripture 57%
Sharing your belief...57%
Praying together 54%
Contributing time and/or money 53%
Working toward an inner sense of peace/ well-being 46%

Quite interestingly, there has been much emphasis in contemporary American Catholic writings on the family as a domestic church, the Church of the home, and in theologian Karl Rahner's words, "the smallest individual church." Papal exhortations have called for restoration of the role of family and family spirituality in church life and for the Church to develop better partnership with today's families. Family life has been called intimate, sacred, and holy, and the Catholic family's essential, spiritual mission to reach out beyond its normal bounds to serve humanity has been articulated with much energy. (*Family Perspective* 20-22 and *Familiaris Consortio* par. 49) Social outreach themes notwithstanding, recent writing on family spirituality often redounds to the family circle, the small "private sphere" community, within which love, support, and the staples of life can be shared.

> The ordinary experiences and activities of family living can and do reveal the sacred. Look at any point within the broad range of our families. Most of the significant human events occur there. Birth and death, marriage and childhood, sickness, and unemployment — these are but a few of the ordinary events of life, and all form a family spirituality...Small, sometimes momentary ways to evoke the sacred in these and many ordinary family events can be created by a family that tries to be sensitive to the inherent holiness of their life together. (Finley 70-71)

The critical moral ecology issues in American family existence (how to effectively re-connect and reintegrate families and family members with the wider church and social community in order to better serve others) must be examined and addressed by contemporary Catholics too.

In general, Americans exhibit much independence in their religious lives. Many say they view their faith and beliefs as something between only God and them. Consistently during the 1980s, one-third of the American people reported an individual religious experience or a moment of religious insight which changed their lives. Many rely on themselves alone or the good lives they lead for self-fulfillment and happiness, rather than organized religion. (Gallup and Castelli, *The People's Religion* 252)

What then would Americans want from their local churches? Above all, they want them to serve people. They want a sense of community and belonging, often to surmount personal loneliness; help and support for families; pastoral staffs they can relate to; less emphasis on money; assistance in finding meaning in their lives; help on how to put faith and morality into practice; understanding of moral and social justice issues; and insights on how to be better parents. "The Church (remains) a family affair," says George Gallup. "Large numbers of young adults who have stayed away from the Church for a number of years return ...when their children are old enough to begin religious instruction." (Gallup and Castelli, *The People's Religion* 253-55)

American Catholics, according to other research by Gallup's organization, give plaudits to their church on its handling of family needs. (Gallup and Castelli, *American Catholic People* 46-51) Much of this might be attributed to satisfaction among certain Catholics (for example, those over sixty-five) with church services. In any case, American Catholics show low approval of their church's dealings with single persons and young people. The Church receives its worst ratings from its members for its poor service to the separated, divorced, and remarried. Many decry the lack of pastoral care for these church members. Clearly many disagree with church doctrine on divorce and remarriage. There is, likewise, great disagreement between church members and the Church on birth control and premarital sex.

Surveys from the mid-1980s seemed to indicate that American Protestants wanted more spiritual-guidance from their church, while American Catholics wanted more practical help. Foremost, for Catholics are aids to becoming better parents, help with moral issues, help in putting faith into action, and help in deepening their relationship with Jesus. Vast numbers of modern Catholics also look for small groups in parishes, more face-to-face relationships at their churches, and more frequent, informal relationships between priests and laypersons. (Gallup and Castelli, *American Catholic People* 52-3)

What is the influence of the family of origin on an individual's religious life and outlook? Recent research on Catholic families has documented that the family system in which one grows up, one's family of origin, and thus all the relationships formed within it, will have a mighty influence on the individual's religious life and outlook. (Greeley, *Religious Imagination* 51) The family of origin affects the religious imagination and experience of children and youth through:

1) the relationship between the parents of the child...
2) the relationship of the parents to one another
3) the religious devotion of both parents, especially if they are very devout
4) the perception by the child of the parent as religiously influential, which presumably indicates the parent's explicit attempt to teach religion. (Greeley, *Religious Imagination* 60)

Another major study reinforces the importance of the family of origin in influencing the religious life and practices of children and youth.

Family factors are also important, particularly in the high school years. Students whose parents are involved in their parish religious education program and students who experience engagement with faith issues as part of family life are more likely than other students to report favorable outcomes (on tests of religious behavior, beliefs, values, and influences). This is an important finding which affirms that families and church-based programs constitute an important partnership. The suggestion here is that programs best affect students when the family is considered part of the religious education team. ...The family that practices faith models a mature faith, and the message does not escape our children. (Kelly, Benson, Donahue 45)

Do parents affect the religious life and future of young people? Yes, all the time. Young people:

> ...watch in fascination the story their parents are telling. The underlying theme of hope or despair, of graciousness or absurdity which runs through the parental story is surely communicated... The religious imagination of young people is powerfully influenced by what goes on in the family of origin. (Greeley, *Religious Imagination* 61)

As we have examined earlier, families of origin, plus all other Catholic families and households today, are undergoing a protracted, cultural time of transition and diversity. Yet, the Catholic family seems to have a noticeable durability and resiliency.

At the outset of the 1980s, one-third of young Catholics were married invalidly, and about 50% of them had married non-Catholics. Many dissented when it came to church doctrines on divorce, birth control, and nonmarital sex. Yet, many did not (and will not) divorce, and they have found ways to navigate the sizeable stresses of the first years of marriage and marital adjustments. There was "considerable residual strength and resourcefulness" in the typical young Catholic family of the 1980s. Continued ministry efforts among those in troubled relationships was obviously needed too. Transmitting "warm religious images" in Catholic family settings was a strong lead-in for prayerfulness, hopefulness, and social commitment among family members, a factor "much stronger than propositional orthodoxy." (Greeley, *Young Catholic Family* 104-107) This is key to individual socialization and family spiritual growth. The most critical and lasting influences on the religious life of the average American Catholic are his or her spouse, the style of the local parish priest, and his or her parents in precisely that order. (Greeley, *American Catholics* 151) Formal Catholic instruction seems to have had little or no impact on the development of a warm, positive religious imagination and religious outlook among young Catholic adults and families.

> If you grow up in a warm family, you are more likely to have "warm" religious imagery; if you have "warm" religious imagery and grew up in a "warm" family, you are more likely to have a "warm" sexual life with your spouse; ...then you will have a "warm" marriage relationship — no matter how cold it may get during the critical years..." (Greeley, *Young Catholic Family* 111)

Greeley hypothesized that marriage/family cycles and devotional cycles are intimately related. To say that young Catholic family members, "Will be back when they need to...", was fault-ridden. In the 1980s some young Catholics returned, some did not. The key factors in young families' spirituality and active religious practices were the stories of God and faith they had inherited from others and their marital relationships, and the interface between these two.

What do we see as trends among American Catholic families at this time? Further studies and surveys in the 1980s have said the official Church, through its ministers and family helpers of the 1990s, should try to be more aware of and more understanding of ongoing changes in the institution called family. Bringing children up in a specific religious tradition is a priority for many parents according to a Gallup poll completed in 1988. Almost 70% of those with children between 4 and 18 said their kids were receiving some form of religious training. (Hellmich 1A) The National Opinion Research Center (NORC) has drawn some other conclusions. Chiefly, the "structures of Catholic family life have not changed as (much as) the Catholic marriage education "experts" so loudly complain... The major changes, however, in the ambiance of American Catholic family life (and the life of families of whatever religion) are rarely noted by the marriage education experts." (Greeley, *Religious Imagination* 206)

In what basic condition do we find the contemporary Catholic family? Research reported in the early 1980s posited:

> The American Catholic family is going through a transition period which seems, to some, to indicate an increase in divorce rates, intermarriages, single parent families, and working wives and mothers. More statistics show, however, that the divorce rate does not vary much by decade. Catholics seem to be only somewhat more likely to seek divorce, and no more likely to become involved in a mixed marriage than their non-Catholic counterparts. (Greeley, *Religious Imagination* 195)

There have been signs of growing tolerance for pre- and non-marital liaisons, working mothers, and fewer births in American Catholic families, in recent years.

Dramatic pronouncements, though, about the grave and dire consequences of single-parenting, working mothers, mixed marriages, and divorce among American Catholics cannot be adequately supported by valid research data. (Greeley, *Religious Imagination* 206) In many cases, such phenomena do add to the transitory problems and challenges faced by certain Catholic families. But it is yet to be substantiated, by researchers, that these phenomena are leading to serious structural alterations in the modern Catholic family across the board. Despite heated warnings, from some current commentators, Catholic perspectives on some sexual behaviors have changed in recent decades, but these changing perspectives and attitudes do not, necessarily, signal full acceptance of sexual promiscuity or total sexual permissiveness.

Awareness of and greater understanding of what is truly occurring in the many Catholic families and households of the 1990s will help family ministers and church helping-agencies respond more effectively, and maybe even lead families themselves and others to more faithfully transmit beliefs and values within family systems.

The religious scene, in the United States, during the 1990s, as a whole should prove to be "more Catholic, more non-western, more Mormon, more unaffiliated and less Protestant than it is today." What other widespread religious trends in America will shape the faith of the changing and diverse U.S. Catholic families and other households during the 1990s?

Faith will hold steady, the institutional church will not be quite so firm, and the population will be more pluralistic than it is today. And Americans will continue to be unique, with an unmatched combination of high levels of education and high levels of religious belief and activity. (Gallup and Castelli *People's Religion* 265)

WORKS CITED:

Anderson, Herbert. *The Family And Pastoral Care*. Philadelphia: Fortress, 1984.

Bellah, Robert N., et al. *Habits of the Heart: Individualism and Commitment in American Life*. San Francisco: Harper, 1985.

Brigman, K.N., "Religion And Family Strengths." *Wellness Perspectives 1* (1984): 3-9.

Exter, Thomas, "The Census Bureau's Household Projections." *American Demographics* 8.10 (October 1986): 44-47 .

Fee, Joan, et al. *Young Catholics*. New York: Sadlier, 1981.

Finley, Mitch and Kathy. *Family Spirituality: The Sacred in the Ordinary*. National Association of Catholic Diocesan Family Life Ministers, 1984.

Gallup, George and Castelli, Jim. *The American Catholic People*. Garden City: Doubleday, 1987.

_____. *The People's Religion: American Faith in the 90's*. New York: Macmillan, 1990.

Glick, Paul, "Fifty Years of Family Demographics: A Record of Social Change." *Journal of Marriage and Family* 50.4 (November 1988): 865-890.

Greeley, Andrew M. *The Young Catholic Family*. Chicago: Thomas More, 1980.

_____. *The Religious Imagination*. New York: Sadlier, 1981.

_____. *American Catholics Since the Council: An Unauthorized Report*. Chicago: Thomas More, 1980.

Greer, Kate. "Are American Families Finding New Strength in Spirituality?" *Better Homes And Gardens* (January 1988): 16-27.

Hellmich, Nanci. "Experts: Start Training In Religion Early." *USA Today* (April 13, 1990): 1A.

Hoge, Dean R. *Converts, Dropouts, and Returnees: A Study of Religious Change Among Catholics*. New York: Pilgrim, 1981.

Kelly, Frank, Peter Benson, and Michael Donahue. *Toward Effective Parish Religious Education for Children and Young People*. Washington, DC: NCEA, 1986.

Naisbitt, John and Aburdene, Patricia. *Megatrends 2000*. New York: Morrow, 1990.

NCCB. *A Family Perspective In Church And Society*. Washington DC: USCC,

1988.

Russell, Cheryl and Exter, Thomas F. "America At Mid-Decade." *American Demographics* 8.1 (January 1986): 22-29.

Santi, Lawrence L. "Change in the Structure and Size of American Households, 1970-1985." *Journal of Marriage and Family.* 49.4 (November 1987): 833-837.

Stinnett, Nick and DeFrain, John. *Secrets of Strong Families.* New York: Berkley, 1985.

Veroff, Joseph, et. al. *The Inner American: A Self-Portrait From 1957-1976,* New York: Basic, 1981.

Waldrop, Judith. "Inside America's Households." *American Demographics* 11.3 (March 1989): 20-27.

Chapter Three

THE FAMILY LIFE CYCLE

Betty Carter and Monica McGoldrick

Our aim in this essay is to provide a view of the life cycle in terms of the inter-generational connectedness in the family. We believe this to be one of our greatest human resources. We do not mean to oversimplify the complexity of life's transitions or to encourage stereotyping by promoting classifications of "normality" that constrict our view of human life. On the contrary, our hope is that by superimposing the family life cycle framework on the natural phenomenon of lives through time, we can add to the depth with which we view family problems and strengths.

The family life cycle perspective frames problems and strengths within the course the family has moved along in its past, the tasks it is trying to master, and the future toward which it is moving. It is our view that the family is more than the sum of its parts. The individual life cycle takes place within the family life cycle, which is the primary context of human development. We think this perspective is crucial to understanding the emotional problems that people develop as they move together through life.

THE FAMILY AS A SYSTEM MOVING THROUGH TIME

We should like to consider the motion of the entire three- or four-generational system as it moves through time. Relationships with parents, siblings (Cicirelli), and other family members go through stages as one moves along the life cycle, just as parent-child and spouse relationships do. It is extremely difficult, however, to think of the family as a whole because of the complexity involved. As a system moving through time, the family has basically different properties from all other systems. Unlike all other organizations, families incorporate new members only by birth, adoption, or marriage, and members can leave only by death, if then. No other system is subject to these constraints. In nonfamily systems, the roles and functions of the system are carried out in a more or less stable way, by replacement of those who leave for any reason, or else the system dissolves and people move on into other organizations. Although families also have roles and functions, the main value in families is in the relationships, which are irreplaceable. If a parent leaves of dies, another person can be brought in to fill a parenting function, but this person can never replace the parent in his or her personal emotional aspects.

Our view is that "family" comprises the entire emotional system of at least three, and now frequently four, generations. This is the operative emotional field at any given moment. We do not consider the influence of the family to be restricted to the members of a particular household or to a given nuclear family branch of the system. Thus although we recognize the dominant American pattern of separately domiciled nuclear families, they are, in our view, emotional subsystems, reacting to past, present, and anticipated future relationships within the larger three-generational family system.

Our three-generational perspective should not be confused with what Goode has referred to as the "classical family of Western nostalgia," a mythological time when the extended family reigned supreme, with mutual respect and satisfaction between the generations (Hess and Waring 303-314). The sexism, classism, and racism of such patriarchal arrangements should not be underestimated. However, we pay a price for the fact that modern families are characterized by choice in interpersonal relationships: whom to marry, where to live, how many children to bear, how to conduct relationships within the nuclear and extended family, and how to allocate family tasks. As Hess and Waring have observed, "As we move from the family of obligatory ties to one of voluntary bonds, relationships outside the nuclear unit similarly lose whatever normative certainty or consistency governed them at earlier times. For example, sibling relationships today are almost completely voluntary, subject to disruption through occupational and geographic mobility, as indeed it might be said of marriage itself" (303). In the past, respect for parents and obligation to care for elders was based on their control of resources, reinforced by religious tradition and normative sanction. Now, with the increasing ability of younger family members to determine their own fates in marriage and work, the power of elders to demand filial piety is reduced. In the past, maintenance of family relationships was understood to be the responsibility of women: they cared for children, they cared for the men, and they cared for the elderly and the sick. This is changing. But our culture is still dedicated to the "individualism" of the frontier and has made no adequate arrangements for society to take up these responsibilities, and many, particularly the poor and the powerless, usually women and children, are falling through the cracks. We are not, however, trying to encourage a return to a rigid inequitable three-generational, patriarchal family, but rather we want to foster a recognition of our connectedness in life — within any type of family structure — with those who went before us and those who follow after. At the same time it is important to recognize that many problems are caused when changes at the social level of the system lag behind changes at the family level, and, therefore, fail to validate and support the changes.

Although family process is by no means linear, it exists in the linear dimension of time. From this we can never escape. Earlier work on the life cycle has rarely taken this complex process adequately into account. Perhaps this is so because, from a multigenerational perspective, there is no unifying task such as can be described if the life cycle stages are limited to descriptions of individual development or parenting tasks. But the tremendous life-shaping impact of one generation on those following is hard to overestimate. For one thing the three or four different generations must accommodate to life cycle transitions simultaneously. While one generation is moving toward older age, the next is contending with the empty nest, the third with young adulthood, forming careers and intimate peer adult relationships and having children, and the fourth with being inducted into the system. Naturally there is an intermingling of the generations, and events at one level have a powerful effect on relationships at each other level. The important impact of events in the grand-parental generation is routinely overlooked when one is focused on the nuclear family. Painful experiences such as illness and death are particularly difficult for families to integrate, and are thus most likely to have a long-range impact on relationships in the next generations, as has been shown in the impressive work of Norman Paul (Paul and Grosser 339-345; Paul and Paul; Brown 457-482).

There is ample evidence by now that family stresses, which are likely to occur around life cycle transition points, frequently create disruptions of the life cycle and produce symptoms and dysfunction. Hadley and his colleagues found that symptom onset correlated significantly with family developmental crises of addition and loss of family members. Walsh and Orfanidis both found that a significant life cycle event (death of a grandparent), when closely related in time to another life cycle event (birth of a child), correlated with patterns of symptom development at a much later transition in the family life cycle (the launching of the next generation). There is growing evidence that life cycle events have a continuing impact on family development over a long period of time.

As illustrated in Chart 1 (see page 42), we view the flow of anxiety in a family as being both "vertical" and "horizontal" (Carter). The vertical flow in a system includes patterns of relating and functioning that are transmitted down the generations of a family primarily through the mechanism of emotional triangling (Bowen). It includes all the family attitudes, taboos, expectations, labels, and loaded issues with which we grow up. One could say that these aspects of our lives are like the hand we are dealt: they are the given. What we do with them is the issue for us.

The horizontal flow in the system includes the anxiety produced by the stresses on the family as it moves forward through time, coping with the changes and transitions of the family life cycle. This includes both the predictable developmental stresses and those unpredictable events, "the slings and arrows of outrageous fortune," that may disrupt the life cycle process (untimely death, birth of a handicapped child, chronic illness, war) Given enough stress on the horizontal axis, any family will appear extremely dysfunctional. Even a small horizontal stress on a family in which the vertical axis is full of intense stress will create great disruption in the system.In our view the degree of anxiety engendered by the stress on the vertical and horizontal axes at the points where they converge is the key determinant of how well the family will manage its transitions through life. It becomes imperative, therefore, to assess not only the dimensions of the current life cycle stress, but also their connections to family themes, triangles, and labels coming down in the family over historical time (Carter).

Although all normative change is to some degree stressful, we have observed that when the horizontal (developmental) stress intersects with a vertical (transgenerational) stress, there is a quantum leap in anxiety in the system. If, to give a global example, one's parents were basically pleased to be parents and handled the job without too much anxiety, the birth of the first child will produce just the normal stresses of a system expanding its boundaries in our era. If, on the other hand, parenting was a cause celebre' of some kind in the family of origin of one or both spouses, and has not been dealt with, the transition to parenthood may produce heightened anxiety for the couple. The greater the anxiety generated in the family at any transition points, the more difficult or dysfunctional the transition will be.

Chart 1
Horizontal and vertical stressors

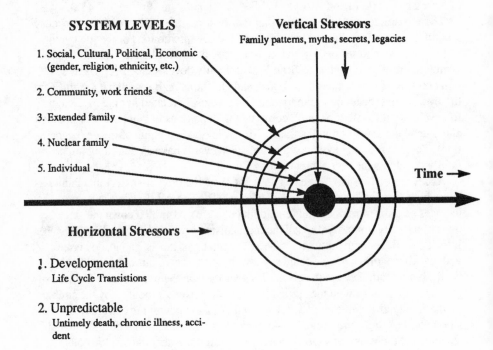

In addition to the stress "inherited" from past generations and that experienced while moving through the family life cycle, there is, of course, the stress of living in this place at this time. One cannot ignore the social, economic, and political context and its impact on families moving through different phases of the life cycle at each point in history. We must realize that there are huge discrepancies in social and economic circumstances between families in our culture, and this inequality has been escalating. At present the top 10% of the population have 57% of the net wealth of the country while the bottom 50% of the population share 4.5% of the total net worth (Thurow 30-37). Among working men only 22% will earn as much as $31,000 and among working women only 3% will earn this much. (Society's treatment of working women is still grossly unequal, with working women earning no more than 65% of what their male counterparts in the work force earn, and with women and children accounting for 17% of those in poverty.) We are rapidly moving to the point where only a family with two full-time working parents will be able to support a middle-class existence (Thurow 30-37).

Cultural factors also play a major role in how families go through the life cycle. Not only do cultural groups vary greatly in their breakdown of life cycle stages and definitions of the tasks at each stage, but it is clear that even several generations after immigration the family life cycle patterns of groups differ markedly (Woehrer 65-78; Gelfand and Kutzik; Lieberman). One must also recognize the strain that the vastly accelerated rate of change puts on families today, whether the changes themselves are for better or for worse.

Even the stages of the life cycle are rather arbitrary breakdowns. The notion of childhood has been described as the invention of 18th-century Western society and adolescence as the invention of the 19th century (Aries), related to cultural, economic, and political contexts of those eras. The notion of young adulthood as an independent phase could easily be argued to be the invention of the 20th century, and for women as independent persons of the late 20th century, if that is accepted even now. The phases of the empty nest and older age are also developments primarily of this century, brought about by the smaller number of children and the longer life span in our era. Given the present rates of divorce and remarriage, the 21st century may become known for developing the norm of serial marriage as part of the life cycle process. Developmental psychology has tended to take an a historical approach to the life cycle. In virtually all other contemporary cultures and during virtually all other historical eras, the breakdown of life cycle stages has been different from our current definitions. To add to this complexity, cohorts born and living through different periods differ in fertility, mortality, acceptable gender roles, migration patterns, education, needs and resources, and attitudes toward family and aging.

THE CHANGING FAMILY LIFE CYCLE

Within the past generation, the changes in family life cycle patterns have escalated dramatically, due especially to the lower birth rate, the longer life expectancy, the changing role of women, and the increasing divorce and remarriage rate. While it used to be that child rearing occupied adults for their entire active life span, it now occupies less than half the time span of adult life prior to old age. The meaning of the family is changing drastically, since it is no longer organized primarily around this activity.

The changing role of women in families is central in these shifting family life cycle patterns. Women have always been central to the functioning of the family. Their identities were determined primarily by their family functions as mother and wife. Their life cycle phases were linked almost exclusively to their stages in child-rearing activities. For men, on the other hand, chronological age has been seen as a key variable in life cycle determinations. But this description no longer fits. Today women are moving through the parenting cycle more rapidly than their grandmothers; they may put off developing personal goals beyond the realm of the family, but they can no longer ignore such goals. Even women who choose a primary role of mother and homemaker must now face an "empty nest" phase that equals in length the years devoted primarily to child care. Perhaps the modern feminist movement was inevitable, as women have come to need a personal identity. Having always had primary responsibility for home, family, and child care, women necessarily began to struggle under their burdens as they came to have more options for their own lives. Given their pivotal role in the family and their difficulty in establishing concurrent functions outside the family, it is perhaps not surprising that women have been the most prone to symptom development at life cycle transitions. For men the goals of career and family are parallel. For women these goals conflict and present a severe dilemma. While women are more positive than men about the prospect of marriage, they are less content than men generally with the reality of it (Bernard). Women, not men, are likely to become depressed at the time of childbirth; this appears to have a great deal to do with the dilemma that this shift creates in their lives. Women, more than men, seek help during the child-rearing years, and as their children reach adolescence and leave home and as their spouses retire or die. And women, not men, have had primary responsibility for older relatives. Surely women's seeking help for problems has much to do with the different ways in which they are socialized, but it also reflects the special life cycle stresses on women, whose role has been to bear emotional responsibility for all family relationships (McGoldrick, *Changing Family Life Cycle* 31-69).

Actually, at an ever-accelerating pace over the decades of this century, women have radically changed — and are still changing — the face of the traditional family life cycle that had existed for centuries. In fact the present generation of young women is the first in history to insist on their right to the first phase of the family life cycle — the phase in which the young adult leaves the parents' home, establishes personal life goals, and starts a career. Historically women were denied this most crucial step in adult development and were handed, instead, from their fathers to their husbands. In the next phase, that of the newly married couple, women are establishing two-career marriages, having children later, having fewer children, or choosing not to have children at all. In the "pressure cooker" phase of the family life cycle — that of families with young children — the majority of divorces take place, many of them initiated by women; in the next phase, that of families with adolescents, couples have the fastest growth in divorce rates at present. It is during this phase that the "midlife crisis" has sent unprecedented numbers of women back to school and work. Finally, when the children are gone, a married couple — if they are still married — can expect an average of 20 years alone together, the newest and longest phase of the family life cycle. In former times one spouse, usually the husband, died within two years of the marriage of the youngest child. Old age, the final phase of the family life cycle, has almost become a phase for women only, both because they outlive men and because they live longer than they used to. At ages 75-79, only 24% of women have husbands whereas 61% of men have wives. At ages 80-84, 14% of women have husbands and 49% of men have wives. At age 85, 6% of women have husbands and 34% of men have wives (Bianchi and Spain; Glick, *Journal of Family Issues* 7-26; U.S. Senate Special Committee Report).

The recent changes in these patterns make our task of defining the "normal" family life cycle even more difficult. An ever increasing percent of the population are living together without marrying (3% of couples at any one point in time), and a rapidly increasing number are having children without marrying. At present 6% or more of the population is homosexual. Present estimates are that 1% of young women will never marry, three times the percent for their parents' generation; 25% will never have children; 50% will end their marriages in divorce and 20% will have two divorces. Thus families often are not going through the "normal" phases at the "normal" times. If one adds to this the number of families that experience the death of a member before old age and those that have a chronically ill or handicapped or alcoholic family member, which alters their life cycle pattern, the number of "normal" families is even smaller. Another major factor affecting all families at one time or another is migration (Sluzki 379-390; McGoldrick, *Ethnicity and Family Therapy*). The break in cultural and family continuity created by migration affects family life cycle patterns for several generations. Given the enormous number of Americans who have immigrated within the last two generations, the percentage of "normal" families is diminished still further.

Thus our paradigm for middle-class American families is currently more or less mythological, though statistically accurate, relating in part to existing patterns and in part to the ideal standards of the past against which most families compare themselves.

It is imperative that we at least recognize the extent of change and variations in the norm that are now widespread and that they help families to stop comparing their structure and life cycle course with that of the family of the 1950s. While relationship patterns and family themes may continue to sound familiar, the structure, ages, stages, and form of the American family have changed radically.

It is time for professionals to give up attachments to the old ideals and to put a more positive conceptual frame around what is: two paycheck marriages; permanent "single-parent" households; unmarried couples and remarried couples; single-parent adoptions; and women of all ages alone. It is past time to stop thinking of transitional crises as permanent traumas, and to drop from our vocabulary words and phrases that link us to the norms and prejudices of the past: children of divorce, out-of-wedlock child, fatherless home, working mother, and the like.

THE STAGES OF THE INTACT MIDDLE-CLASS AMERICAN FAMILY LIFE CYCLE

Our classification of family life cycle stages of American middle-class families in the last quarter of the 20th century highlights our view that the central underlying process to be negotiated is the expansion, contraction, and realignment of the relationship system to support the entry, exit, and development of family members

Chart 2a
The Stages of the Family Life Cycle

Family Life Cycle Stage	Emotional Process of Transition: Key Principles
1. Leaving home: Single young adults	Accepting emotional and financial responsibility for self
2. The joining of families through marriage: The new couple	Commitment to new system
3. Families with young children	Accepting new members into the system
4. Families with adolescents	Increasing flexibility of family boundaries to include children's independence and grandparents' frailties
5. Launching children and moving on	Accepting a multitude of exits from and entries into the family system
6. Families in later life	Accepting the shifting of generational roles

in a functional way. We offer suggestions about the process of change required of families at each transition. (*See chart above*)

THE LAUNCHING OF THE SINGLE YOUNG ADULT

In outlining the stages of the family life cycle, we have departed from the tradi-

Chart 2b
The Stages of the Family Life Cycle

Second-Order Changes in Family Status Required to Proceed Developmentally

a. Differentiation of self in relation to family of origin
b. Development of intimate peer relationships
c. Establishment of self in work and financial independence.

a. Formation of marital system
b. Realignment of relationships with extended families and friends to include spouse

a. Adjusting marital system to make space for child(ren)
b. Joining in childrearing, financial, and household tasks
c. Realignment of relationships with extended family to included parenting and grandparenting roles

a. Shifting of parent-child relationships to permit adolescents to move in and out of the system
b. Refocus on mid-life marital and career issues
c. Beginning shift toward joint caring for older generation

a. Renegotiation of marital system as a dyad
b. Development of adult-to-adult relationships between grown children and their parents
c. Realignment of relationships to include in-laws and grandchildren
d. Dealing with disabilities and death of parents (grandparents)

a. Maintaining own and/or couple functioning and interests in face of physiological decline; exploration of new familial and social role options
b. Support for a more central role of middle generation.
c. Making room in the system for the wisdom and experience of the elderly, supporting the older generation without overfunctioning for them
d. Dealing with loss of spouse, siblings, and other peers and preparation for own death; life review and integration

tional sociological depiction of the family life cycle as commencing at courtship or marriage and ending with the death of one spouse. Rather, considering the family to be the operative emotional unit from the cradle to the grave, we see a new family life cycle beginning at the stage of "young adults," whose completion of the primary task of coming to terms with their family of origin most profoundly influences who, when, how, and whether they will marry and how they will carry out all succeeding stages of the family life cycle (Aylmer 191-208). Adequate completion of this requires that the young adult separate from the family of origin without cutting off or fleeing reactively to a substitute emotional refuge. Seen in this way, the "young adult" phase is a cornerstone. It is a time to formulate personal life goals and to become a "self" before joining with another to form a new family subsystem. The more adequately young adults can differentiate themselves from the emotional program of the family of origin at this phase, the few vertical stressors will follow them through their new family's life cycle. This is the chance for them to sort out emotionally what they will take along from the family of origin what they will leave behind and what they will create for themselves. As mentioned above, of greatest significance is the fact that until the present generation this crucial phase was never considered necessary for women, who had no individual status in families. Obviously the tradition of caretaking has had profound impact on the functioning of women in families, as the current attempt to change the tradition is now also having.

We have found it useful to conceptualize life cycle transitions as requiring second-order change, or change of the system itself. Problems within each phase can often be resolved by first-order change, or a rearranging of the system, involving an incremental change. We have summarized the shifts in status required for successful accomplishment of life cycle transitions in column 2 of Chart 2, which outlines the stages and tasks of the life cycle. In our view it is important not to become bogged down with a family in first-order details when they have not made the required second-order shifts in relationship status to accomplish the tasks of the phase.

In the young adult phase, problems usually center on either young adults' or their parents' not recognizing the need for a shift to a less hierarchical form of relating, based on their now all being adults. Problems in shifting status may take the form of parents' encouraging the dependence of their young adult children, or of young adults' either remaining dependent or rebelling and breaking away in a pseudo-independent cutoff of their parents and families.

For women, problems at this stage more often focus on short-circuiting their definition of themselves in favor of finding a mate. Men more often have difficulty committing themselves in relationships, forming instead a pseudo-independent identity focused around work.

It is our view, following Bowen, that cutoffs never resolve emotional relationships and that young adults who cut off their parents do so reactively and are in fact still emotionally bound to rather then independent of the family "program." The shift toward adult-to-adult status requires a mutually respectful and personal form of relating, in which young adults can appreciate parents as they are, needing neither to make them into what they are not nor to blame them for what they could not be. Neither do young adults need to comply with parental expectations and wishes at their own expense. Only when the generations can shift their status relations and reconnect in a new way can the family move on developmentally.

THE JOINING OF FAMILIES THROUGH MARRIAGE: THE COUPLE

The changing role of women, the frequent marriage of partners from widely different cultural backgrounds, and the increasing physical distances between family members are placing a much greater burden on couples to define their relationship for themselves than was true in traditional and precedent-bound family structures (McGoldrick, *Changing Family Life Cycle* 212-236). While any two family systems are always different and have conflicting patterns and expectations, in our present culture couples are less bound by family traditions and freer than ever before to develop male-female relationships unlike those they experienced in their families of origin. Marriage tends to be misunderstood as a joining of two individuals. What it really represents is the changing of two entire systems and an overlapping to develop a third subsystem. As Jessie Bernard pointed out long ago, marriage represents such a different phenomenon for men and for women that one must really speak of "his" and "her" marriage. Women tend to anticipate marriage with enthusiasm, although statistically it has not been a healthy state for them. Men, on the other hand, approach marriage typically with much ambivalence and fear of being "ensnared," but, in fact, do better psychologically and physically in the married state than women. Marriage has traditionally meant the wife taking care of the husband and children, providing for them a haven from the outside world. The traditional role of "wife" provides low status, no personal income and a great deal of work for women and typically has not met women's needs for emotional comfort. This is part of the reason for the recent lowering rate of marriage and later age of marriage, as well as the trend for women to delay child bearing, or even to choose not to have children at all. A rise in women's status is positively correlated with marital instability and with the marital dissatisfaction of their husbands. When women used to fall automatically into the adaptive role in marriage, the likelihood of divorce was much lower. In fact it appears very difficult for two spouses to be equally successful and achieving. There is evidence that either spouse's accomplishments may correlate negatively with the same degree of achievement in the other. Thus achieving a successful transition to couplehood in our time, when we are trying to move toward the equality of the sexes (educationally and occupationally), may be extraordinarily difficult (McGoldrick, *Changing Family Life Cycle* 212-236).

Although we hypothesize that failure to renegotiate family status is the main reason for marital failure, it appears that couples are very unlikely to present extended family problems as the stated issue. Problems reflecting the inability to shift family status are usually indicated by defective boundaries around the new subsystem. In-laws may be too intrusive and the new couple afraid to set limits, or the couple may have difficulty forming adequate connections with the extended systems., cutting themselves off in a tight twosome. At times the inability to formalize a living together couple relationship in marriage indicates that the partners are still too enmeshed in their own families to define a new system and accept the implications of this realignment. (Bradt 235-255)

It is useful in such situations to help the system to move to a new definition of itself (second-order change) rather than to get lost in the details of incremental shifts they may be struggling over (sex, money, time).

BECOMING PARENTS: FAMILIES WITH YOUNG CHILDREN

The shift to this stage of the family life cycle requires that adults now move up a generation and become caretakers to the younger generation. Typical problems that occur when parents cannot make this shift are struggles with each other about taking responsibility, or refusal or inability to behave as parents to their children. Often parents find themselves unable to set limits and exert the required authority, or they lack the patience to allow their children to express themselves as they develop. Often, parents with children at this phase are somehow not accepting the generation boundary between themselves and their children. They may complain that their four-year-old is "impossible to control." Or, on the other hand, they may expect their children to behave more like adults, reflecting too strong a generational boundary or barrier. In any case, child centered problems are typically addressed by helping parents gain a new of themselves as part of a new generational level with specific responsibilities and tasks in relation to the next level of the family.

The central struggle of this phase, however, in the modern two-paycheck (and sometimes two-career) marriage is the disposition of child-care responsibilities and household chores when both parents work full-time. The pressure of trying to find adequate child care when there is no satisfactory social provision for this family need produces serious consequences: the two full-time jobs may fall on the women; the family may live in conflict and chaos; children may be neglected or sexually abused in inadequate child-care facilities; recreation and vacations may be sharply curtailed to pay for child care; or the women may give up her career to stay home or work part-time. This problem is at the center of most marital conflict presented at this stage, and often leads to complaints of sexual dysfunction and depression. It is not possible to work successfully with couples at this phase without dealing with the issues of gender and the impact of sex-role functioning that is still regarded as the norm for most men and women. It is not really surprising that this is the family life cycle phase that has the highest rate of divorce.

The shift at this transition for grandparents is to move to a back seat from which they can allow their children to be the central parental authorities and yet form a new type of caring relationship with the grandchildren. For many adults this is a particularly gratifying transition, which allows them to have intimacy without the responsibility that parenting requires.

THE TRANSFORMATION OF THE FAMILY SYSTEM IN ADOLESCENCE

While many have broken down the stages of families with young children into different phases, in our view the shifts are incremental until adolescence, which ushers in a new era because it marks a new definition of the children within the family and of the parents' role in relation to their children. Families with adolescents must establish qualitatively different boundaries than families with younger children, a job made more difficult in our times by the lack of built-in rituals to facilitate this transition (Quinn et al. 101-112). The boundaries must now be permeable. Parents can no longer maintain complete authority. Adolescents can and do open the family to a whole array of new values as they bring friends and new ideals into the family arena. Families that become derailed at this stage may be rather closed to new values and threatened by them and they are frequently stuck in an earlier view of their children. They may try to control every aspect of their lives at a time when, developmentally, this is impossible to do successfully. Either the adolescent withdraws from the appropriate involvements for this develr the parents become increasingly frustrated with what they perceive as their own importance. For this phase the old Alcoholics Anonymous adage is particularly apt for parents: "May I have the ability to accept the things I cannot change, the strength to change the things I can, and wisdom to know the difference." Flexible boundaries that allow adolescents to move in and be dependent at times when they cannot handle things alone, and to move out and experiment with increasing degrees of independence when they are ready, put special strains on all family members in their new status with one another. This is also a time when adolescents begin to establish their own independent relationships with the extended family, and it requires special adjustments between parents and grandparents to allow and foster these new patterns.

Families need to make the appropriate transformation of their view of themselves to allow for the increasing independence of the new generation, while maintaining appropriate boundaries and structure to foster continued family development.

The central event in the marital relationship at this phase is usually the "midlife crisis" of one or both spouses, with an exploration of personal, career, and marital satisfactions and dissatisfactions. There is usually an intense renegotiation of the marriage, and sometimes a decision to divorce. This is not to say that common adolescent symptoms, such as drug and alcohol abuse, teenage pregnancy, or delinquency or psychotic behavior, should not be carefully assessed and dealt with.

FAMILIES AT MIDLIFE:
LAUNCHING CHILDREN AND MOVING ON

This phase of the family life cycle is the newest and the longest, and for these reasons, it is in many ways the most problematic of all phases (McCullough and Rutenberg 287-311). Until about a generation ago, most families were occupied with raising their children for their entire active adult lives until old age. Now, because of the low birth rate and the long life span of most adults, parents launch their children almost 20 years before retirement and must then find other life activities. The difficulties of this transition can lead families to hold on to their children or can lead to parental feelings of emptiness and depression, particularly for women who have focused their main energies on their children and who now feel unprepared to face a new career in the work world. The most significant aspect of this phase is that it is marked by the greatest number of exits and entries of family members. It begins with the launching of grown children and proceeds with the entry of their spouses and children. It is a time when older parents are often becoming ill or dying. This, in conjunction with the difficulties of finding meaningful new life activities during this phase itself, may make it a particularly difficult period. Parents not only must deal with the change in their own status as they make room for the next generation and prepare to move up to grandparental positions, but also with a different type of relationship with their own parents, who may become dependent, giving them (particularly women) considerable caretaking responsibilities. This can also be a liberating time, in that finances may be easier than during the primary years of family responsibilities and there is the potential for moving into new and unexplored areas — travel, hobbies, new careers. For some families this stage is seen as a time of fruition and completion and as a second opportunity to consolidate or expand by exploring new avenues and new roles. For others it leads to disruption, a sense of emptiness and overwhelming loss, depression, and general disintegration. The phase necessitates a restructuring of the marital relationship now that parenting responsibilities are no longer required.

THE FAMILY IN LATER LIFE

As Walsh (312-332) has pointed out, few of the visions of old age we are offered in our culture provide us with positive perspectives for healthy later-life adjustment within a family or social context. Pessimistic views of later life prevail. The current myths are that most elderly people have no families; that those who do have families have little relationship with them and are usually set aside in institutions; or that all family interactions with older family members are minimal. On the contrary, the vast majority of adults over 65 do not live alone but with other family members. Over 80% live within an hour of at least one child (Walsh 312-332).

Another myth about the elderly is that they are sick, senile, and feeble and can best be handled in nursing homes or hospitals. Only 4% of the elderly live in institutions and the average age at admission is 80. There are indications that if others did not foster their dependence or ignore them as functional family members, even this degree of dependence would be less.

Among the tasks of families in later life are adjustments to retirement, which not only may create the obvious vacuum for the retiring person, but may put a special strain on a marriage that until then has been balanced in different spheres. Financial insecurity and dependence are also special difficulties, especially for family members who value managing for themselves. And, while loss of friends and relatives is a particular difficulty at this phase, the loss of a spouse is the most difficult adjustment, with its problems of reorganizing one's entire life alone after many years as a couple and of having fewer relationships to help replace the loss. Grandparenthood can, however, offer a new lease on life, and opportunities for special close relationships without the responsibilities of parenthood.

Difficulty in making the status changes required for this phase of life are reflected in older family members' refusal to relinquish some of their power, as when a grandfather refused to turn over the company or make plans for his succession. The inability to shift status is reflected also when older adults give up and become totally dependent on the next generation, or when the next generation does not accept their lessening powers or treats them as totally incompetent or irrelevant. The evidence suggests that men and women respond very differently to their roles in aging and this too must be carefully assessed (Hesse-Biber & Williamson 261-278).

Even when members of the older generation are quite enfeebled, there is not really a reversal of roles between one generation and the next, because parents always have a great many years of extra experience and remain models to the next generations for the phases of life ahead. Nevertheless, because older age is totally devalued in our culture, family members of the middle generation often do not know how to make the appropriate shift in relational status with their parents.

Helping family members recognize the status changes and the need for resolving their relationships in a new balance can help families move on developmentally.

MAJOR VARIATIONS IN THE FAMILY LIFE CYCLE

DIVORCE AND REMARRIAGE

While the statistical majority of the American middle and upper classes still go through the traditional family life cycle stages as outlined above, the largest variation from that norm consists of families in which divorce has occurred. With the divorce rate currently at 50% and the rate of redivorce at 61% (Glick, *American Demographics* 21-25), divorce in the American family is close to the point at which it will occur in the majority of families and will thus be thought of more and more as a normative event. In our experience as clinicians and teachers, we have found it useful to conceptualize divorce as an interruption or dislocation of the traditional family life cycle, which produces the kind of profound disequilibrium that is associated throughout the entire family life cycle with shifts, gains, and losses in family membership (Peck and Manocherian 335-371; Ahrons and Rodgers 187-205). As in other life cycle phases, there are crucial shifts in relationship status and important emotional tasks that must be completed by the members of divorcing families in order for them to proceed developmentally. As in other phases, emotional issues not resolved at this phase will be carried along as hindrances in future relationships (Peck and Manocherian 335-371).

Therefore, we conceptualize the need for families in which divorce occurs to go through one or two additional phases of the family life cycle in order to restabilize and go forward developmentally again at a more complex level. Of women who divorce, at least 35% do not remarry. These families go through one additional phase and can restabilize permanently as post-divorce families (Brown 372-401). The other 65% of women who divorce remarry, and these families can be said to require negotiation of two additional phases of the family life cycle before permanent restabilization (Carter and McGoldrick 402-429).

Our concept of the divorce and postdivorce family emotional process can be visualized as a roller-coaster graph, with peaks of emotional tension at all transition points:

1. At the time of the decision to separate or divorce
2. When this decision is announced to family and friends
3. When money and custody/visitation arrangements are discussed
4. When the physical separation takes place
5. When the actual legal divorce takes place
6. When separated spouses or ex-spouses have contact about money or children
7. As each child graduates, marries, has children or becomes ill
8. As each spouse is remarried, moves, becomes ill, or dies.

These emotional pressure peaks are found in all divorcing families — not necessarily in the above order — and many of them take place over and over again, for months or years. A more detailed depiction of the process appears in Chart 3. (See pages 56-57)

The emotions released during the process of divorce relate primarily to the work of emotional divorce — that is, the retrieval of self from the marriage. Each partner must retrieve the hopes, dreams, plans, and expectations that were invested in this spouse and in this marriage. This requires mourning what is lost and dealing with hurt, anger, blame, guilt, shame, and loss in oneself, in the spouse, in the children, and in the extended family.

Families in which the emotional issues of divorce are not adequately resolved can remain stuck emotionally for years, if not for generations. The predictable peaks of emotional tension in the transition to remarriage occur at the time of serious commitment to a new relationship; at the time a plan to remarry is announced to families and friends; at the time of the actual remarriage and formation of a stepfamily, which takes place simultaneously and as the logistics of stepfamily life are put into practice.

The family emotional process at the transition to remarriage consists of struggling with fears about investment in a new marriage and a new family: one's own fears, the new spouse's fears, and the children's fears (of either or both spouses); dealing with hostile or upset reactions of the children, the extended families, and the ex-spouse; struggling with the ambiguity of the new family structure, roles, and relationships; rearousal of intense parental guilt and concerns about the welfare of children; and rearousal of the old attachment to ex-spouse (negative or positive). Chart 4 depicts the process in somewhat greater detail. (See pages 58-59)

THE FAMILY LIFE CYCLE OF THE POOR

The adaptation of multiproblem poor families to a stark political, social and economic context has produced a family life cycle pattern that varies significantly from the middle-class paradigm so often and so erroneously used to conceptualize their situation. Hines (515-544) offers a thought-provoking breakdown of the family life cycle of the poor into three phases: the "unattached young adult" (who may actually be 11 or 12 years old), who is virtually on his or her own, unaccountable to adults; families with children — a phase that occupies most of the life span and commonly includes three- and four-generation households; and the phase of the non-evolved grandmother, still involved in a central childrearing role in old age — still actively in charge of the generations below.

ETHNICITY AND THE FAMILY LIFE CYCLE

Most descriptions of the typical family life cycle (including ours) fail to convey the considerable effects of ethnicity and religion on all aspects of how, when, and in what way a family makes its transitions from phase to phase. Although we may ignore these variables for the theoretical clarity of focus on our commonalities, those working with real families in the real world cannot afford to ignore this. The definition of "family," as well as the timing of life cycle phases and the importance of different transitions, varies depending on a family's cultural background. It is essential for those working with families to consider how ethnicity intersects with the life cycle and to encourage families to take active responsibility for carrying out the rituals of their ethnic or religious group(s) to mark each phase. It is also extremely important for us to help families develop rituals that correspond to the actual transitions of their lives, including those transitions that the culture has not validated.

Ethnicity interacts with the family life cycle at every stage. Families differ in their definition of "family", in their definition of the timing of life cycle phases and the tasks appropriate at each phase, and in their traditions, rituals, and ceremonies to mark life cycle transitions. When cultural stresses or transitions interact with life cycle transitions, the problems inherent in all change are compounded. In fact Plath (1981) has argued that the very definition of human development in Eastern cultures is different from Western cultures in beginning with the definition of a person as a social being and defining development as by growth in the human capacity for empathy and connection. By contrast Western cultures begin with the individual as a psychological being and define development as growth in the human capacity for differentiation.

Ethnicity patterns our thinking, feeling, and behavior in both obvious and subtle ways, although generally operating outside of our awareness. It plays a major role in determining what we eat, how we work, how we relate, how we celebrate holidays and rituals, and how we feel about life, death, and illness. We see the world through our own cultural filters and we often persist in our established views in spite of clear evidence to the contrary.

Ethnicity as used here refers to a concept of a group's "peoplehood" based on a combination of race, religion, and cultural history, whether or not members realize their commonalities with each other. It describes a commonality transmitted by the family over generations and reinforced by the surrounding community. But it is more than race, religion, or national and geographic origin, which is not to minimize the significance of race or the special problem of racism. It involves conscious and unconscious processes that fulfill a deep psychological need for identity and historical continuity. It unites those who conceive of themselves as alike by virtue of their common ancestry, real or fictitious, and who are so regarded by others.

The consciousness of ethnic identity varies greatly within groups and from one group to another. Families vary in attitude toward their ethnicity as a result of clannishness, regressive holding on to past traditions, and fear of changing cultural norms, on the one hand, to denial of any ethnic values of patterns, on the other. In groups that have experienced serious prejudice and discrimination, such as Jews and

Chart 3a
Dislocations of the Family Life Cycle
Requiring Additional Steps to Restabilize and Proceed Developmentally

Divorce Phase	Emotional Process of Transition: Prerequisite Attitude
1. The decision to divorce	Acceptance of inablility to resolve marital tensions sufficiently to continue relationship
2. Planning the breakup of the system	Supporting viable arrangements for all parts of the system
3. Separation	a. Willingness to continue cooperative coparental relationship and joint financial support of children b. Work on resolution of attachment to spouse
4. The divorce	More work on emotional divorce: Overcoming hurt, anger, guilt, etc.

Post Divorce Phase	Emotional Process of Transition: Prerequisite Attitude
1. Single-parent (custodial household or primary residence)	Willingness to maintain financial responsibilities, continue parental contact with ex-spouse, and support contact of children with ex-spouse and his or her family
2. Single-parent (noncustodial)	Willingness to maintain parental contact with ex-spouse and support custodial parent's relationship with children

Blacks, family attitudes about allegiance to the group may become quite conflicted and members may even turn against each other, reflecting prejudices in the outside world. Some groups have a choice about ethnic identification whereas others, because of their color or other physical characteristics, do not. Ethnicity intersects with class, religion, politics, geography, the length of time a group has been in this country, the historical cohort, and the degree of discrimination the group has experienced. Generally speaking, Americans tend to move closer to the dominant American value system as they move up in class. People in different geographic locations evolve new cultural norms. Religion also modifies or reinforces certain cultural values. Families

Chart 3b
Dislocations of the Family Life Cycle
Requiring Additional Steps to Restabilize and Proceed Developmentally

Developmental Issues

Acceptance of one's own part in the failure of the marriage

a. Working cooperatively on problems of custody, visitation, and finances
b. Dealing with extended family about the divorce

a. Mourning loss of intact family.
b. Restructuring marital and parent-childe relationships and finances; adaptation to living apart
c. Realignment of relationships with extended family; staying connected with spouses's extended family

a. Mourning loss of intact family: giving up fantasies of reunion
b. Retrieval of hopes, dreams, expectations from the marriage
c. Staying connected with extended families

Developmental Issues

a. Making flexible visitation arrangements with ex-spouse and his family
b. Rebuilding own financial resources
c. Rebuilding own social network

a. Finding ways to continue effective parenting relationship with children
b. Maintaining financial responsibilities to ex-spouse and children
c. Rebuilding own social network

that remain within an ethnic neighborhood, who work and socialize with members of their group, and whose religion reinforces ethnic values, are likely to maintain their ethnicity longer than those who live in a very heterogeneous setting and have no social reinforces of their cultural traditions. The degree of ethnic intermarriage in the family also plays a role in cultural patterns (McGoldrick & Preto, 1984).
Nevertheless, there is burgeoning evidence that ethnic values and identifications are retained for many generations after immigration and play a significant role in family life throughout the life cycle. Second-, third-, and even fourth-generation Americans differ from the dominant culture in values, behavior, and life cycle patterns.

Chart 4a
Remarried Family Formation: A Developmental Outline

Steps	Prerequisite Attitude
1. Entering the new Relationship	Recovery from loss of first marriage (adequate "emotional divorce")
2. Conceptualizing and planning new marriage and family	Accepting one's own fears and those of new spouse and children about remarriage and froming a stepfamily Accepting need for time and patience for adjustment to complexity and ambiguity of : 1. Multiple new roles 2. Boundaries: space, time, membership, and authority. 3. Affective Issues: guilt, loyalty conflicts, desire for mutuality, unresolvable past hurts
3. Remarriage and reconstitution of family	Final resolution of attachment to previous spouse and ideal of "intact" family; Acceptance of a different model of family with permeable boundaries

When we talk of families moving through the life cycle together, it is important to note how our clients themselves define "family." For example, the dominant American (primarily WASP) definition has focused on the intact nuclear family, including other generations often only to trace the family genealogy to distinguished ancestors who were in this country before 1776, or for southern WASP families, noting family members who took part in the Civil War (McGill & Pearce, 1982). For Italians, by contrast, one might even say there is no such thing as the "nuclear family." For this group family has tended to refer to the entire extended network of aunts, uncles, cousins, and grandparents, who are all involved in family decision making, who share holidays and life cycle transition points together, and who tend to live in close proximity, if not in the same house (Rotunno & McGoldrick, 1982). Black families tend to focus on a wide informal network of kin and community in their even broader definition of family, which goes beyond blood ties to close long-time friends, who are considered family members (Stack, 1975; Hines & Boyd, 1982). The Chinese go even further, to include all their ancestors and all their descendents in their definition of family. Everything they do is done in the context of this entire family group and reflects on it, bringing shame or pride to the entire set of generations. It should be added, however, that women

Chart 4b
Remarried Family Formation: A Developmental Outline

Developmental Issues

Recommitment to marriage and to forming a family with readiness to deal with the complexity and ambiguity

a. Work on openness in the new relationships to avoid pseudomutality
b. Plan for maintenance of cooperative financial and coparental relationships with ex-spouses
c. Plan to help children deal with fears, loyalty conflicts, and membership in two systems
d. Realignment of relationships with extended family to include new spouse and children.
e. Plan maintenance of connections for children with extended family of ex-spouses(s).

a. Restructuring family boundaries to allow for inclusion of new spouse-stepparent.
b. Realignment of relationships and financial arrangements throughout subsystems to permit interweaving of several systems.
c. Making room for relationships of all children with biological (noncustodial) parents, grandparents, and other extended family.
d. Sharing memories and histories to enhance stepfamily integration.

in Asian families have traditionally been moved into their husband's family at the time of marriage, and their names disappear from the family tree in the next generation, leaving only the males as permanent members of a family (Kim et at., 1981; Kim, 1985). Thus, in a sense, Asian families consist of all one's male ancestors and descendents.

IMMIGRATION AND THE LIFE CYCLE

Migration is so disruptive in itself that we could say it adds an entire extra stage to the life cycle for those families who must negotiate it. The readjustment to a new culture is by no means a single event, but is a prolonged developmental process of adjustment that will affect family members differently, depending on the life cycle phase they are in at the time of the transition.

Families' attitudes toward ethnicity depend on many factors, such as how much time has passed since immigration, their life cycle stage at the time of immigration, and the circumstances that led them to migrate: did they come alone as young adults, or as young children with their nuclear family, or in their later years as part of a mass migration because of political or economic oppression? All who migrate must deal with conflicting cultural norms of the country of origin and of the United States. A person's cultural identity will depend on his or her facility with the new language; economic and political situation; flexibility in making new connections with work, friends, and organizations such as church, schools, government bureaucracies, and the health-care system; and remaining connections to the country of origin. Immigrants may wall off the past, forcing their children to speak English only and never talking about the country they left behind. Or they may wall off the new culture, living and working in an ethnic enclave, never making an effort to learn English or to negotiate the American system. A third approach is to attempt to assume a pattern of biculturality, passing on to their children stories and traditions and at the same time learning the ways of the new culture.

People who migrate in the young-adult phase may have the greatest potential for adapting to the new culture in terms of career and marital choices. However, they are perhaps the most vulnerable to cutting off their heritage, leaving themselves open to emotional isolation at later phases of the life cycle when the need for cultural support and identification tends to increase (Gelfand & Kutzik 1979). The result is that they may be permanently cut off, unable to maintain continuity between heritage and children.

Families that migrate with young children are perhaps strengthened by having each other, but they are vulnerable to the reversal of generational hierarchies. If the family migrates with small children (even more so with teenagers), there is a likelihood that the parents will acculturate more slowly than their children, creating a problematic power reversal in the family (Lappin & Scott 1982). If the children must take on the task of interpreting the new culture for the parents, parental leadership may be so threatened that children are left without effective adult authority to support them and without a positive identification with their ethnic background to ease their struggle with life in this new culture. Helping the younger generation to show respect for the values of the older generation is usually the first step in negotiating such conflicts. Families that migrate at this phase may also have problems down the road, particularly at the launching phase where the children feel guilty about leaving parents who are not at home in the culture.

Families migrating when their children are adolescents may have more difficulty because they will have less time together as a unit before the children move out on their own. Thus the family must struggle with multiple transitions and generational conflicts at once. In addition, the distance from the grand-parental generation in the old country may be particularly distressing as grandparents become ill, dependent, or die. The parents may experience severe stress in not being able to fulfill their obligations to their parents in the country of origin. It is not uncommon for symptoms to develop in adolescents in reaction to their parents' unexpressed distress.

Sometimes if the first generation is older at the time of immigration and lives in an ethnic neighborhood in the new country, its conflicts of acculturation may be postponed. The next generation, particularly in adolescence, is likely to reject the ethnic values of parents and strive to become "Americanized" (Sluzki 1979). Intergenerational conflicts often reflect the value struggles of families in adapting to the United States. Members of the third or fourth generation are usually freer to reclaim aspects of their identities that were sacrificed in the previous generations because of the need to assimilate.

Any life cycle transition can trigger ethnic identity conflicts since it puts families more in touch with the roots of their family traditions. How the rituals of transition are celebrated can make an important difference in how well the family will adjust to the changes (See Friedman's essay in Chapter 4 of this volume). All situational crises—divorce, illness, job loss, death, retirement—can compound ethnic identity conflicts causing people to lose a sense of who they are.

CONCLUSIONS

In conclusion, we direct the reader's thoughts toward the powerful (and preventive) implications of family life cycle celebration: those rituals, religious or secular, that have been designed by families in every culture to ease the passage of its members from one status to the next. As Friedman points out, all family relationships in the system seem to unlock during the time just before and after such events, and it is often possible to shift things with less effort during these intensive periods than could ordinarily be expended in years of struggle. (See Friedman's essay in Chapter 4 of this volume.)

WORKS CITED

Ahrons, C. H. "Joint Custody Arrangements in the Postdivorce Family." *Journal of Divorce* (1980) 3:187-205.

Ahrons, C. R. H. and Rogers, R. *The Divorced Family.* New York: Norton, 1987.

Aries, P. *Centuries of Childhood: A Social History of Family Life.* New York: Vintage, 1962.

Bernard, J. *The Future of Marriage.* New York: Bantam, 1972.

Bianchi, S. M. and Spain, D. *American Women in Transition.* New York: Russel Sage, 1986.

Bowen, M. *Family Therapy in Clinical Practice.* New York: Aronson, 1978.

Butler, R.N. and Lewis, M.I. (1983). *Aging and mental health.* New York: New American Library.

Bradt, Jack O. "Becoming Parents: Families with Young Children". *The Changing Family Life Cycle.* Ed. Betty Carter and Monica McGoldrick. Boston: Allyn, 1989. 235-255.

Brown, Freda Herz. "The Impact of Death and Serious Illness on the Family Life Cycle". *The Changing Family Life Cycle.* Ed. Betty Carter and Monica McGoldrick. Boston: Allyn, 1989. 457-482.

Carter, E.A. "The Transgenerational Scripts and Nuclear Family Stress: Theory and Clinical Implications." *Georgetown Family Symposium.* Ed. R.R. Sager. Vol. 3. Washington, DC: Georgetown, 1975-76.

Carter, Betty and Monica McGoldrick, editors. *The Changing Family Life Cycle.* Boston: Allyn, 1989.

Cicirelli, V. G. "Sibling Relationships throughout the Life Cycle." *The Handbook*

of Family Psychology and Therapy. Ed. L. L'Abate. Homewood, IL: Dorsey,
  1985.
Gelfand, D. E., and Kutzik, A. J., editors. *Ethnicity and Aging*. New York:
  Springer, 1979.
Glick, P. "How American Families are Changing." *American Demographics*
  January 1984: 21-25.
Glick, P. "Marriage, Divorce, and Living Arrangements." *Journal of Family Issues*
  5.1 (1984): 7-26.
Goode, W. J. *World Revolultion and Family Patterns*. New York: Free Press, 1963.
Hadley, T., et al. "The Relationship Between Family Crises and the Appearance of
  Symptoms in a Family Member." *Family Process* 13 (1974): 207-214.
Hess, B. B. and J. M. Waring. "Changing Patterns of Aging and Family Bonds in
  Later Life." *The Family Coordinator* 27.4 (1984): 303-314.
Hesse-Biber, S., and J. Williamson. "Resource Theory and Power in Families: Life
  Cycle Considerations." *Family Process* 23.2 (1984): 261-278.
Hines, Paulette Moore. "The Family Life Cylce of the Poor." *The Changing
  Family Life Cycle*. Ed. Betty Carter and Monica McGoldrick. Boston: Allyn,
  1989. 515-544.
Hine, Paulette Moore and Franklin Boyd. "Black Families." *Ethnicity and Family
  Therapy*. Ed. M. McGoldrick, J. K. Pearce, and J. Giordano. New York:
  Guilford, 1982.
Kim, Bok-Lim. "Women and Ethnicity." *Presentation at the American Family
  Therapy Association*, June 1985.
Kim, Bok-Lim, et al. *Women in Shadows*. LaJolla, CA: National Committee
  Concerned with Asian Wives of U.S. Servicemen, 1981.
Lappin, J and S. Scott. "Intervention in a Vietnamese Refugee Family." *Ethnicity
  and Family Therapy*. Ed. M. McGoldrick, et al. New York: Guilford, 1982.
Lieberman, M. "Adaptational Patterns in Middle Aged and Elderly: The Role of
  Ethnicity." *Gerontological Society Conference*. Portland, Oregon, October
  1974.
McCullough, Paulina and Sandra Rutenberg. "Launching Children and Moving
  On." *The Changing Family Life Cycle*. Ed. Betty Carter and Monica
  McGoldrick. Boston: Allyn, 1989. 285-310.
McGill, D. and J.K. Pearce. "British American Families." *Ethnicity and Family
  Therapy*. Ed. M. McGoldrick, J. K. Pearce, and J. Giordano. New York:
  Guilford, 1982.
McGoldrick, Monica. "Overview." *Ethnicity and Family Therapy*. Ed. M.
  McGoldrick, et al. New York: Guilford Press, 1982.
McGoldrick, Monica. "Women and the Family Life Cycle." *The Changing Family
  Life Cycle*. Ed. Betty Carter and Monica McGoldrick. Boston: Allyn, 1989.
  31-68.
McGoldrick, Monica and N.G. Preto. "Ethnic Marriage: Implications for
  Therapy." *Family Process* 23 (3): 347-362
McGoldrick, M., et al. *Women in Families: A Framework for Family Therapy*.
  New York: Norton (in press).

Orfanidis, M. "Some Data on Death and Cancer in Schizophrenic Families." *Georgetown Presymposium*. Washington, DC, 1977.

Paul, N. and G. Grosser. Operational Mourning and Its Role in Conjoint Family Therapy." *Community Mental Health Journal* 1 (1965): 339-345.

Paul, N. and B.B. Paul. *A Marital Puzzle*. New York: Norton, 1974.

Plath, D. "Of Time, Love and Heroes." *Adult Development through Relationships*. 1981.

Quinn, W. H., et al. "Rites of Passage in Families with Adolescents." *Family Process* 24.1 (1985): 101-112.

Peck, Judith Stern and Jennifer Manocherian. "Divorce in the Changing Family Life Cycle." *The Changing Family Life Cycle*. Ed. Betty Carter and Monica McGoldrick. Boston: Allyn, 1989. 335-370.

Rotunno, M and Monica McGoldrick. "Italian Families." *Ethnicity and Family Therapy*. Ed. M. McGoldrick, et al. New York: Guilford, 1982.

Sluzki, C. "Migration and Family Conflict." *Family Process* 18.4 (1979): 379-390.

Stack, C. All Our Kin. New York: Harper, 1975.

Thurow, L. "The Surge in Inequality." *Scientific American* 256.5 (1987): 30-37.

U.S. Senate Special Committee on Aging and American Association of Rertired Persons. "Aging America." Washington, DC: U. S. Government Printing Office, 1985.

Walsh, F. "Concurrent Grandparent Death and the Birth of a Schizophrenic Offspring: An Intriguing Finding." *Family Process* 17 (1978): 457-463.

———. "The Family in Later Life." The Changing Family Life Cycle. Ed. Betty Carter and Monica McGoldrick. Boston: Allyn, 1989. 311-332.

Woehrer, C. E. "The Influence of Ethnic Families on Intergenerational Relationships and Later Life Transitions." *Annals of the American Academy of PSS* 464 (Nov. 1982): 65-78.

Chapter Four

A FAMILY APPROACH TO
LIFE CYCLE CEREMONIES

Edwin H. Friedman

It was the congregation's tradition to have the father bless the bar mitzvah child, but here was the maternal grandfather trying to take the place of his dead son-in-law. The boy's father had died five years ago during his older brother's bar mitzvah. The older brother had gone through with his part all right, but he never came into the synagogue again. Now he was back, sitting between his mother, still in mourning, and his 16-year-old sister, once an innocent, pleasant child, but now caught up in an undisciplined life of drugs and sex. Then I spotted the dead father's own aged mother. She had been sitting next to him when he keeled over at the older son's bar mitzvah.

Soon I realized that all the grandparents were bawling. I'd better do something quick, I thought. But I held back. This was a family event, I kept saying to myself. Like so many rites of passage, it was a way of marking change. So I psychologically nailed my shoes to the floor and did not intervene. After a while grandfather regained his composure. Here and there a sniffle, but not much more. He spoke easily now, mentioned his deceased son-in-law, and then directed his grandson to focus on his own future.

When the service was over, you could sense that something had happened. There was rejoicing. It was somewhat subdued, but it was clean of emotional holdovers. I don't really believe in spooks, or devils. But I think I was present at an exorcism.

Life-cycle ceremonies capture the healing process of therapeutic encounter better than any other form of religious experience. Weddings, funerals, and the rites associated with birth and puberty are ancient in form, yet have the most modern results. "Rites of passage," were the first human efforts to deal with modern psychotherapy's major areas of concern: change and separation. They were the first modes of therapy, and originally, as well as today, they are really family therapy. In fact, both their antiquity and their context suggest that the original form of all therapy was family therapy. We seem to have lost sight of this fact because the emphasis in modern healing is on personality and psychodynamics. And this loss has deprived the clergy of valuable opportunities for understanding how family emotional processes operate during these significant moments, as well as how to take advantage of such opportunities to help families heal themselves, and how to encourage family involvement so as to heighten the spirituality of the occasion.

At no other time can we so effectively fulfill the pastoral part of our ministry without having to adopt modes and metaphors from outside our calling. And, at no other time are the two major dimensions of our healing potential so apparent: the uniqueness of our entree into family life, and the power inherent in our community position.

But more than healing is involved. A family approach to life-cycle events also enhances the holiness inherent in the tradition, because religious values are far more likely to be heard when family process is working toward the success of the passage, rather than against it. After all, it is hard to get the message of consecration across at a baptism, a christening, or a bris if there has been intense conflict over the name to be bestowed. Working through the family emotional issues behind such conflicts will enhance the spirituality of the occasion.

This chapter will present a family systems perspective of life-cycle celebrations. It will show how the ceremonies surrounding such nodal occasions in an individual's life may be conceived as family events. It will demonstrate how a family perspective offers practical ways to modify the stress usually accompanying such moments. And it will illustrate how a family systems view of rites of passage leads naturally to creative directions for evolving our own religious traditions without sacrificing the time-hallowed heritage of our past. The framework of this chapter will be to explore four natural life cycle events (death, marriage, pubescence, birth), and then to comment on three nodal events that are less a natural part of the life cycle and more a creation of the times in which we live (divorce, retirement, geographical uprooting).

A FAMILY VIEW OF LIFE-CYCLE EVENTS

Rites of passage are usually associated with emotionally critical moments of life. Yet most studies of these ceremonies have tended to ignore the crucial role of the family at such events. The convention in the social sciences has been to place primary focus on the culture that provides the rites or on the individuals who are being passed through to a new stage in their life cycle. The role of the family on such occasions has tended to be seen as secondary, as occupying more of an intermediary position between the individual members to be passed and society. From this perspective the family participates in the customs provided by a culture as a way of helping its members take their new position in that culture.

Twenty years of experience as a clergyman and family therapist have given me an almost totally different perception of the role of families in rites of passage. I have found that the family, far from being an intermediary, is the primary force operating at such moments - primary not only in that it, and not the culture, determines the emotional quality of such occasions (and therefore the success of the passage), but also in that it is the family more than the culture that ultimately determines which rites are to be used. Families are far less determined by their culture's customs and ways of doing things than they are selective, according to their own characteristics and pathology, of their culture's ceremonial repertoire. (Friedman, *Ethnicity and Family Therapy*).

Indeed, so central is the role of family process in rites of passage that it is probably correct to say it is really the family that is making the transition to a new stage of life at such a time rather than any "identified member" focused upon during the occasion.

What may be the most significant, however, in switching one's primary focus to the family is that it enables one to see the enormous therapeutic potential inherent in natural family crises. The one phenomenon that has stood out in my experience with families of all cultures is that the periods surrounding rites of passage function as "hinges of time."

All family relationship systems seem to unlock during the months before and after such events, and it is often possible to open doors (or close them) between various family members with less effort during these intensive periods than could ordinarily be achieved with years of agonizing efforts.

I believe this is true because, with respect to timing, life cycle events are not as random as they appear. Rather they are usually the coming to fruition or culmination of family processes that have been moving toward those ends for some time. Life cycle events are always part of "other things going on." They always indicate movement, and it is simply easier to steer a ship when it is afloat, even if it is drifting in the wrong direction, than when it is still aground.

Before beginning our discussion of life-cycle events, however, I would like to discuss how confusing the rite with the ceremony inhibits forming a family process view of rites of passage. I will also propose four principles about the relationship of family process to rites of passage that are basic to my conceptualization.

THE RITE OF PASSAGE IS MORE THAN THE CEREMONY

The assumption that the ceremony is the rite of passage inhibits a family view of rites of passage. After all, some individuals are married long before the ceremony, and some never do leave home. Some family members are buried long before they expire and some remain around to haunt for years, if not generations. This myth has a corollary, which is that the members of the family who are the focus of the ceremony are the only ones who are going through the passage. The whole family goes through the passage at nodal events in the life cycle, and the passage often begins months before and ends months after the ceremony.

Ceremonies celebrate. From an emotional systems point of view, they are not in themselves efficacious. Rather, their effect is determined by what has already been developing within the emotional system of the family. Ceremonies do focus the events, however, in that they bring family members into conscious contact with one another and in that they bring processes to a head.

On the other hand, therefore, the celebration event itself can be a very useful occasion for meeting people, for putting people together, for reestablishing relationships, for learning about the family (both by observation and by the hearing of tales), for creating transitions, as in leadership, or for the opportunity to function outside or against one's normal role.

On the other hand, my experience with rites of passage suggests that the more important time for becoming involved with one's family is in the months before and after the celebration, using the event more as an excuse for reentry. Though, naturally, the more one prepares the soil before the celebration, the richer the harvest will be at the event itself.

For example, it would be nice to use the state of flux in a family system usually present at a funeral to bring a brother and sister into verbal communication again. But this is more likely to happen at the funeral if one initiates communication with each of them while the family member to be buried is dying.

Perhaps the most important point to be made about distinguishing the ceremony from the passage is that the potential for change that I have found near nodal family events could not be that great if the event were just the event.

The notion feeds back into itself. If you can get things going right before any given ceremony, then all the natural healing processes that age old traditions have captured in their rites of passage will take over, and at the celebration, do much of your work for you. Elsewhere I have been developing this theme for clergy of all faiths, suggesting that an awareness of family process can enable a minister to draw on the natural strengths in families to enrich religious experience. The idea is not to psychologize religion. Rather the thesis is that when clergymen facilitate the meaningful involvement of family members at life cycle ceremonies, they are in fact allowing natural healing processes to flow, and doing what religion had always intuited but what modern times has come to be called therapy.[1]

PRINCIPLES REGARDING RITES OF PASSAGE

Giving up this myth leads to some very useful principles, which in turn lead to the observation of confirming patterns. For the other side of the notion that the rite of passage is more than the ceremony, and the individuals going through the passage are more than those identified with the ceremony, is the idea that the rites of passage always indicate significant movement in a family system. Therefore, not only can a family approach to rites of passage make them smoother journeys, but the crisis these events precipitate become golden opportunities for inducing change in otherwise stable dysfunctional relationship patterns. As mentioned earlier, family systems seem to unlock during these periods.

On the basis of my experience with families of many cultures, I would assert the following principles regarding rites of passage for families regardless of cultural background.

1. Rites of passage are family events that arise at the time they do because of emotional processes that have been at work in the nuclear and extended family of the member(s) who is (are) the focus of the ceremony.
2. The ceremony or the event itself reflects the fact that processes in the family have been undergoing change and are in a state of flux.

3. The ceremony and the time before and after it are therefore opportune periods for inducing change in the family system.
4. There seem to be certain "normal" time periods for the change and working through of emotional processes at times of life cycle transition, and attempts to hasten or shorten those periods unduly are always indications that there are important unresolved issues in the family relationship system.

This last principle leads to the observation of certain patterns. The incredible similarity in the way the first three principles appeared, no matter what the culture, made me realize I was observing something natural and organic to the human phenomenon. Then it became clear that a key to understanding families not only in the midst of a rite of passage, but at any time, was to note in the family history how the family had functioned at past rites of passage as per indication of the major issues in the family. While it is not possible to pinpoint the exact range of "normality," and how culture will affect the norms, enough of a range may be established to create a benchmark for judging the extremes.

In Chart 1 (see page 68) are seven continua describing time periods around the rites of passage of marriage, birth, and divorce. The center column represents a range that, I have found most people fall within when they are objectively considering the decision to make a change. This is the benchmark period. It is not meant to be all-inclusive, and perhaps could be seen as a slide rule that might expand or contract between the extremes, depending on the culture. What is important is not how exact this column is but what it points to in each direction. On the basis of my experience, I would say that to the extent that members of a family come near those extremes, they are making decisions more with their guts than with their heads and there are important unworked-out issues still to be resolved with the family of origin.

The table also suggests that the opposite extremes say something similar. I emphasize this because these opposite extremes may show up in different generations or different siblings, but reflect similar patterns.[2]

I am in no way saying, however, that families with members who fall on the extremes in one scale will necessarily fall on the extremes in the other scales. It is important to realize also that these continua should not be taken too literally. They are designed primarily to create a tool for gaining perspective and will be less specifically accurate at any given point along the line, though more generally accurate as one moves toward the extremes. (*Warning*: Anyone caught trying to rate himself or herself by means of these "scales" will be considered to have fallen off the ends completely.) While the scales still need refinement, I think the model may hold, even if it makes it appear that some families have members going through life holding one end of their umbilical cord in their hand, looking for someone else to plug it into, or the reverse, as when family members are unable to commit themselves to anyone.

What can be said about individuals who tend to operate near the extremes is that they come from families that have trouble elasticizing their relationships, by which I mean they have difficulty maintaining different distances with a person over time. They tend to control their feelings with on/off switch - it is all or nothing. Other clues have tended to show this also. For example, when either no one or everyone is invited to an event, it may say something similar. And with regard to funerals, cremation hints the same sort of difficultly in allowing the pain of emotional processes to operate naturally. Generally speaking, anything that shows a rush to replace loss or an inability to fill the gap indicates a lack of flexibility in the system.

But the most important ramification of these findings for a family approach to rites of passage is, I believe, that in their universality they support the notion that the human species has developed rites of passage out of its own nature. Traditions, no matter what the culture, reflect or capture this, and ultimately that is why in the

Chart 1

EXTREME	BENCHMARK PERIOD	EXTREME
1. Age when married:		
teenage elopement	21-27	no marriage or mid-forties
2. Length of courtship:		
love at first sight—10 days	6 months to 1 year	five years of going steady or living together
3. Length of engagement:		
eloping right after decision	3-6 months	many years of putting it off
4. Time to birth of first child:		
pregnancy before marriage	2-3 years	childless for whatever reason
5. Time between separation and divorce:		
attempt to hasten legal limits	1-2 years after legal limits	till death do us part
6. Time between separation from one mate and going steady with future mate:		
affair with future mate	2-4 years	withdrawal, promiscuity
7. Time between divorce and remarriage:		
same as examples 5 & 6	2-5 years	same as examples 5 and 6

from *The Curvature of Emotional Space*

emotional life of any family, the rites of passage through the life cycle are ideal times for learning about the family, as well as for helping it to heal itself. (For the application of these concepts to entire organizations, see Friedman, *Generation to Generation*.)

FOUR NATURAL RITES OF PASSAGE

The following discussion covers four natural rites of passage — funerals, weddings, puberty rites, and birth — and includes examples of how a family approach can make the passage less fraught with anxiety, and even turn it into an opportunity for helping the family in broader terms. I also comment later on three nodal points in the modern life cycle that are not as natural but are becoming so widespread as to approach traditional rites of passage in emotional significance — divorce, retirement, and geographical uprooting.

FUNERALS

I begin with an event that is usually considered to mark the end of the life cycle because death is undoubtedly the single most important event in family life. Over the years I have seen more change in families - marriage, divorce, pregnancy, geographical moves, other deaths - occur within a year after the death of a family member than after any other nodal point in the life cycle. Another reason for beginning with the end is that this event, especially if it is associated with a particularly important member of the family, can influence the celebration of other nodal events that follow. For example, at the first wedding, baptism, bar mitzva, and so on, following the death of a person important to the system, there is likely to be a larger turnout than one might have been otherwise led to expect. When that occurs the phenomenon itself may give an indication of who is going to replace the deceased member of the family. On the other hand, the turnout for a funeral appears less likely to be influenced by the nodal events that preceded it.

Death creates a vacuum, and emotional systems, as physical systems, will rush to fill it. In the process cutoffs between family members will begin and end, and freedom and getting stuck will be the fate of others. Shifts in responsibility are normal, and replacement becomes a goal for many. The fluidity of a system around the time of death is thus also greater, though not necessarily for an indefinite period. In other words, if one is going to take advantage of that period, the funeral, its preparations, and its "celebration" can be a crystalizing experience. And while there may be more anxiety and pain for the family when a death is expected, such cases offer more opportunity for change. Six major kinds of opportunity become available during this rite of passage:

1. The chance to take or shift responsibility;
2. The opportunity to reestablish contact with distant relatives (or close relatives who live at a distance);
3. The opportunity to learn family history;
4. The chance to learn how to deal with the most anxious forces that formed one's emotional being;

5. Though this may subsume the previous, the opportunity to shift energy directions in the family triangles, all of which seem to resurrect themselves at
   such moments;
6. The opportunity to reduce the debilitating effects of grief.

The last has the character of a time warp, since it involves affecting what
usually comes after death by what one does in the family before death. But it may
be the most crucial one of all, and better than any other notion it encapsulates the
idea that a rite of passage is more than a ceremony. The basic notion is: grief is the
residue of the unworked-out part of a relationship.[3]

Several of these are exemplified by the following story, in which I was involved
as clergyman, but where I was able to use my knowledge of family process to let
flow the natural healing forces released by rites of passage.

A woman who was very involved in community mental health called and
asked if I would be willing to do a "nonreligious" funeral for her husband,
a renowned scientist, aged 46, who was terminally ill and might die any
day. The rub was that she didn't want him to know about it. He was very
areligious, but she wanted to do this for her sons, ages 19 and 12. I replied
that I couldn't agree to do a funeral for a man while he was still alive
unless I could meet him. (There were additional reasons for my taking this
position, having to do with my general ideas that secrecy almost always
stabilizes dysfunction and increases anxiety in a system. I concluded this
after observing numerous clients in therapy where the impending death of
a loved one was handled in a hush-hush way.)[4]

The woman said that meeting her husband was out of the question, and I
just said, "Think it over." She called back later that day to say that she had
spoken to her husband and he had agreed to meet with me. I told her that I
did not want to see him alone, but with her and her two sons. She agreed,
but warned me that she did not want any therapy. I said I would only ask
questions.

The husband had just come back from the hospital to die at home. When I
arrived he was lying in bed, and while physically weak, was perfectly
lucid. He was an only child, and kept a phone next to his bed so that when
his aged parents called from the Midwest, they would not realize how bad
things really were.

The older son was there, but I was informed that the younger son, who had
asthma, had been sent to the home of his mother's mother. I began by
telling the dying man (in front of his wife and son) that I had never met
anyone who knew he was going to die, and wondered what he thought
about it. He responded in a self-denying way, seemingly trying to convey
that he was approaching his end with perfect equanimity. I pushed the
point by saying that his wife had said he was a very nonreligious man, and
I wondered if he was now hedging his bet before he met his maker. He

again responded lucidly and with a great sense of character, "No." He knew this was really going to be final. I then asked him what he wanted said at his funeral. (I already told him that I had found some passages from Albert Einstein that I thought would be appropriate, but I was now speaking in terms of a eulogy.) He then replied with amazing humility that there was nothing particular about himself that he wanted emphasized.

As far as I was concerned, to this point all the questions were just "probing the line." I now turned to the son and asked him in front of his father what he wanted said at his father's funeral. At this point, by the way, a fortuitous ringing of the phone took the mother out of the room; she never came back in. I proceeded to catalyze a conversation of the most personal kind between father and son over the issue of what was to be said at father's funeral. The man died the next day. The son, at my urging, wrote and delivered the eulogy, and the mother, several days later sent me a long thank-you note and a copy of Kubler-Ross's *On Death and Dying.*[5]

As a clergyman I had an unusual opportunity in this situation, but I think that what happened there could only have occurred in that family during such a rite of passage. Such experience clarified for me that there are ways of encouraging such a process if you are "lucky" enough to be seeing a client around the time of a death in the family.

My own experience with the dying, the dead, and their survivors is that it is not an individual who is dying as much as it is a member of a family - that is, part of an organism is dying. When this focus is maintained, as impersonal and cold as it may seem at first, many new ways of seeing things unfold. For example, using the principle of extremes mentioned before, I believe that where extraordinary efforts are made, either to end the person's life, "to reduce suffering," or to prolong a person's life when he or she is biologically alive but existentially dead, the family either is desirous of rushing through the passage or fearful of entering it. In either case it will say something about the family and the importance of the dying person to it at that moment. Such an approach also refocuses the so-called ethical issues around the "right to die."

There is another important way in which the focus on the dying person, rather than the family, misguides this rite of passage: it requires that the dying be compuis mentis. In many cases such persons are psychotically senile, unconscious, in a coma, obstreperously denying, or hopelessly confused. In those situations, from the point of view of that individual's existence, the person "might as well be dead." But that is in no way true from the point of view of the family. As long as the dying person is above ground, he or she is a live part of the organism. (Compare the extraordinary efforts to keep political leaders alive even though they are no longer capable of ruling.) Systems know the extraordinary significance of burial.

WEDDINGS

If death is the most portentous event in family life, marriage may be the most symptomatic in two senses. First, my experience with over 2000 couples before marriage has led me to the conclusion that the timing of weddings is far from random. I have found, for example, that many couples either meet their spouse or decide to marry within six months of a major change in the family of origin of one of the partners. It is not that romance does not count, but simply that it is not enough to move a relationship to marriage. Weddings can also be symptomatic of family process in that stresses surrounding the engagement and wedding preparation period seem really to make the seams show. This can be true with funerals also, but there are some major differences. More likely than not, death will have an implosive effect on a family, in which all the members pull together, even if after the funeral they fight over the inheritance. With weddings one must decide whether to invite those one does not want to be with and the burden of choice can become almost overbearing, depending on how many sides one is trying to please. Whereas with a funeral the need for comfort makes the closest relatives willing to be with one another, with a wedding the desire to be joyous makes some of those same relatives anathema. Another major difference between weddings and funerals is that in death one is dealing with the loss of an insider whereas with marriage the problem is the inclusion of an outsider - despite the old saw, "I am not losing a daughter but gaining a son."

Some families handle such transition situations with amazing perceptiveness. One man who was marrying a woman with a five-year-old daughter turned to the little girl immediately after the pronouncement and also gave the child a ring. He knew what he was doing; under those circumstances he really did marry both, and not only his bride.

One of the aspects of family ceremonies that has always appalled me, and yet has also proved to me that the unseen family process has more power than the ceremony, is the loss of critical taste at family events. I have performed very sloppy weddings in the most uncomfortable settings (bees literally in my bonnet) and had everyone come up afterward to congratulate me on the warmest wedding they have ever attended. But I have also been part of such anxious systems that even in the most elaborately arranged settings, the most eloquent homilies were ignored and I had all I could do to keep from inadvertently stepping on the bridal gown and tripping the bride.

As an opportunity for inducing change, I have found that the rite of passage surrounding a wedding is the most propitious for redirecting focus. The opportunities for learning about the family and reworking triangles described with regard to funerals are there also, but the time around weddings stands out primarily as the time to redirect a parent's focus, and once again crisis is opportunity.

Though this is clearly the case, most couples who experience difficulties with their parents over a wedding see this period as just something to be gotten through until they can get married and get away. This avoidance of the experience might be similar to cremation after death. Of course, the real getting away only occurs if the young people use that period to develop more differentiation of self in the relationships with their parents. And again, couples who are experiencing pain at such moments (as with terminal deaths) may be more fortunate. Where problems arise in the family of origin during wedding preparations, the opportunities for redirection of focus are plentiful.[6]

To begin with, I can say categorically that I have never seen a religious, social, or other issue worked out regarding a marital choice where the efforts have been made directly on the content of the issue. For example, if parents are critical of the marital choice on the ground of different religious or social backgrounds, efforts to change the parents' minds by saying such things as, "But Mom, you were always so liberal yourself," or "Dad, you always taught me to treat everyone equally," are doomed to failure. I have seen many a bride or groom spend an entire weekend with critical parents trying to show them how illogical their views were and, leave in the belief that they had changed their parents' minds, only to receive a letter later in the week showing that they were back at ground zero. These efforts to deal with the content of the parents' complaint are ineffective because one is dealing with symptom, not cause. The cause of almost all severe parental reactions to marital choice is the failure of the reacting parent to have worked out something important in other relationships. The focus has been misplaced. On the other hand, I have found almost 100% success in reducing the significance of such issues, if not eliminating them altogether, when the bride or groom is able to refocus the reacting parent on his or her own parents.

Three major factors are always present in the reacting relative's position in the family:

(1) he or she is having great difficulty differentiating from the child getting married

(2) not necessarily distinct from this, the child getting married is very important to the balance of the parents' marriage

(3) that parent or relative is caught up in some emotionally responsible position in his or her own family of origin.

The key, however, no matter which way of refocusing one chooses, is that an impending wedding is a sign of a relationship system in flux. Some members are going to feel the pull of the forces of change more than others. Who is going to react most depends on who stabilized his or her own life through some kind of emotional dependence on the person getting married. For example, some parents use a child as an anchor to keep from getting drawn back into the vortex of the parents' parents' pull. Or they invest in a child to compensate for the absence of affection in a marriage. The road to no change at such moments is to elope, cut off, or try to placate the parents as much as possible until one gets married and can start one's own family. Those approaches guarantee a transference of emotional intensity into the new family being formed. But where individuals can be taught to seize the opportunity at the rite of passage of a wedding, they leave a lot of unnecessary baggage at home.

The wedding as a rite of passage is like the movement of an iceberg, with most of what is in motion unseen by the human eye.

PUBESCENCE

The third most universal rite of passage is that of puberty, the onset of adulthood. Of the four this one has lost much of its family significance in modern culture, becoming associated often with cultural phenomena, graduations, dating, and so on. My own religious tradition, of course, has maintained it with the celebration of the bar (boy) or bat (girl) mitzva. I would like to shift gears in this section and talk with my own tradition's metaphor about this rite of passage.[7]

The major reason I wish to stay within my own tradition here is that I have experience with changes in the tradition based on what I have learned about family process, and the results have been both astounding and enlightening. What I wish to show is, first, how something as obviously individual, no less child focused, is really very much a family rite; and second, how making everyone aware of that fact actually increases the effectiveness of the passage. There are other lessons that come forth also - that the message of the emotional system is a more powerful medium than the culture tradition, establishing it or perverting it; and that, old traditions, even without articulation of family process, have recognized it all the time.

The Jewish tradition of bar mitzva (literally, son of, or worthy of, the commandments) is at least 1500 years old. On a day close to a boy's 13th birthday, he is called up to bless the scripture reading or to read a portion. From the point of view of traditional Jewish law, he is now an adult able to give witness in court, be responsible for his own wrongdoing, and be counted as one of the ten men needed for a public service (minyon). In the 1920s (around the time of the 19th amendment, which gave women the right to vote), progressive branches of Judaism introduced bat mitzva for a girl, though the ceremony has only become widespread only recently, since the renaissance of the women's movement.

Today, from the religious point of view, depending on the branch of Judaism, the ceremony can be just the scripture blessing, a reading of the portion in Hebrew, which the child may have just memorized, or a rite with more emphasis on the meaning of the portion, with the child giving more than a stereotyped thank-you speech and, adding a talk that interprets his portion.

In terms of contemporary sociology, the bar mitzva, especially for the Jews of middle-class suburbia, often appears to be an event of great social importance. In some places it has been joked, "The bar has become more important than the mitzva." And it might be added, "The caterer more important than the rabbi."

But in either case, from the family process point of view, the ceremony always appears to be child focused. The first time I began to think of bar mitzva in family terms was actually before I had trained to do family therapy. I was doing some work as a community relations specialist for the White House. For the first time in my life, I began to sense the pressures non-Jews feel around Christmas time. Colleagues I had worked with all year began to become extremely anxious. They began to shop compulsively for gifts beyond their means, and drinking became more frequent. Then one Friday evening, as I was leaving a staff Christmas party on my way to a weekend that was to include a bar mitzva, things seemed strangely familiar. The anxiety, the gift giving, the drinking - there was something the two had in common. Years later when I had the conceptual framework I began to understand. It was the force of family togetherness: All the family intensity, the problems with relatives, the unspoken feelings, the pressure to relate that many individuals spend much of a year trying to avoid, become unavoidable for a Christian near Christmas; for Jewish families something similar occurs around a bar mitzva. As I began to explore this notion, other events and findings propelled me further in that direction of observing family force fields. First, a father of a bar mitzva boy (unbeknownst to me, in line for a transplant) went into heart failure during his son's service, and died. He was an only child, sitting next to his widowed, terribly dependent mother at that time. This experience led me to an extraordinary amount of additional information. As I related what had happened to others, I began to hear an incredible number of reports about parents going into dysfunction near the time of a sons' bar mitzva, including suicides, breakdowns, and other forms of physical illness. (It is, of course, well known that the suicide rate goes up nationally in later December.)

I began to put things together. No wonder I had never been really successful in calming a bar mitzva child's anxiety no matter how well prepared he was. It was not his anxiety I was dealing with. No wonder mothers whom I had previously perceived to be models of efficiency and astute reasonableness approached me almost on the verge of hysteria in seeking bar mitzva dates. No wonder fathers running top government agencies and used to living with daily crises seemed to go limp at this period. I was dealing with phenomena with far-ranging effects.

Since I knew that a most effective means of dealing with panic was to offer an alternative mode of behavior, I immediately hit upon involving the family members more in the ceremony and the preparation. I soon found to my surprise and delight that these efforts had more reward than I expected.

The first change I made was in the method of choosing the portion. Traditionally there is no choice; one goes by the calendar cycle. I began to meet with the child, learn a little about him and his family, add what I already knew, and then make several suggestions based on interest and style, leaving it to the child and parents to make final selections. Then I had a study session with the entire family — parents, siblings, grandparents, if they were in town — in which discussion (even argument) was promoted about interpretation. At the end of the discussion, the child was given the charge that he would be the teacher for the day. He was told to divide his talk into three parts - a synopsis in his own words of the portion, his interpretation of what the Biblical author was trying to say, and any interpretations he wished to make for the day.

After the family meetings, I continued to meet with the bar mitzva child several times to help with the writing of his talk, but I began to assume less responsibility. Whereas in former days I used to become terribly concerned about the articulation, coherence, and overall conceptualization of the talk, I was now primarily concerned to ask questions (which I wanted taken back to the family) that helped with the development of the ideas.

Soon I realized that my role had changed significantly. Instead of bearing the burden of helping this child through his rite of passage, I had a team on which I was more a coach than the star player. With that in mind, I also began to make changes in the ceremony. First I stopped giving my sermon myself other than an introduction, which described the development of bar mitzva in Jewish tradition and its further shaping by our congregation. The child was called "our teacher for today," and the father (or, in some cases, both parents) was asked to bless the child, publicly or privately. Since the congregation had a tradition of creative services from the beginning, families started creating their own services. Continuing with my role as coach, I would make available source books, ask for about six to ten passages, and then take responsibility for fitting them into the prayer order. Families, of course, differed in the extent to which I could select, some becoming so involved that they printed, at their own expense, a supplement that even contained the scripture portion itself in Hebrew and English, and artistic members of the family (sometimes the child himself) began to create designs for the cover. Sometimes a sibling wrote a poem for a frontpiece. One family had a coat of arms that went back for generations and decorated the cover with that.

All families were given the option of having the bar mitzva at home if they chose. Sometimes musical members of the family played an overture or background music during the silent prayer. A musical child might play on a guitar or trumpet a tune he or she had created for the service. The parents also gave out portions of the service to incoming relatives, who read them to the congregation. Blessings over the meal were distributed also, each family being encouraged to allot these responsibilities as seemed natural.

The results have been beyond what I could have foreseen. Family anxiety seems greatly reduced, there is much less focus on materialistic expression, and, despite less direct involvement by me, the child generally does a better overall performance. In other words, though I have been trying less to "teach" the child myself, whatever process has been released by the transfer of my functioning to the family is also producing more thoughtful, deeper intellectual efforts on the part of the child. Finally, though I am less "out front," I seem to get more thanks than before from visiting relatives. The systems seem to know.

BIRTH

The fourth natural rite of passage celebrated by all religious tradition is the birth of a child. It is discussed after funerals and weddings because, in the life of a family, it comes in the middle of things; and it sometimes culminates more than it initiates. As with other nodal events, the significance of birth to a family, and the future position of the celebrated, has to do with what has been happening a year either side of the event, which is not the birth date, but the gestation period. The important period, therefore, is from a year before conception to a year after the birth. Sometimes, because of the replacement phenomenon, the emotional processes that culminate in a birth may have been percolating for generations.

Thus, while birth itself is a very short passage, in family terms it can be the longest and, as with other passages, this nodal event always indicates the system is in flux. Understanding birth in terms of family emotional process can help in the ceremonies during this passage.

If the atmosphere before some weddings is reminiscent of the American Indian gauntlet rite, what happens in some families during pregnancy reminds one of the celestial portents in Shakespeare or in the Testaments that presage a significant advent.

Birth can have an immediate impact on the family. The sudden emotional investment in the newborn (or the fetus) can break up a previously stable marriage.

It can give a mother more (false) security for facing life, her husband, or her own mother. It can result in a sibling of the newborn becoming ill, depressed, or dysfunctional. In one family, for example, a very adaptive wife became extremely self-possessed as soon as she felt the baby within her. Her autocratic, apparently independent husband developed almost overnight a fatty (benign) tumor. Some similar disruption of homeostasis may be suspected where fathers are killed in auto accidents or run away during their wives' pregnancies.

The negative effects of the birth are not caused by the actual birth itself. It is rather that a new family member is joining a system whose stability was precarious to begin with. Generally, at the time of a birth, the more free-floating anxiety that exists, the more unresolved emotional attachment, the more distance between the parents, the more triangled and older sibling in the parents' relationship, then the more likely the "blessed event" will either upset the balance of things or bring about a new homeostasis. In the former case, tensions and symptom(s) will eventually surface; in the latter, the newborn may be the one who will eventually suffer years later when it tries to get out of homeostatic patterns it had unwittingly stabilized by its entrance. A family approach to the life cycle suggests that a post-partum depression of mother can be deferred for 20 years and then slow up in the child when it tries to separate (become more a-*part*).

Just as decisions to marry can be deeply embedded in the emotional processes of the family, so also can "decisions" to have children. An extraordinary number of "accidents" (conception) can be seen as far from serendipitous when viewed in the context of the parents' nuclear and extended families around the time of conception. For example, children who come long after a family has been completed tend to assume they were accidents. But they usually come as a replacement—perhaps to fill a hole in mother's empty nest. What percentage of the human race was planned in any generation? What matters is not whether or not a child was conceived with conscious planning, but whether or not the parents decided to "adopt" this accident as their own.

THREE NODAL LIFE CYCLE EVENTS

Funerals, weddings, births, and the onset of puberty have been universal rites of passage as long as the human species has had culture. Our modern culture seems to be producing three other nodal points of great consequence for the life cycle: divorce, retirement, and geographical uprooting. I should like to discuss these changes as family events also. However, I wish to make clear that I think there is an important difference between these three and the former four. The former are all connected to the life cycle biologically. They are part of being human. It is not as clear to me that in themselves the latter have the same power for change, unless perhaps they are, as is often the case, residuals of the former events — for example, where the divorce, or at least the separation, came within a year after an important death; or the geographical move soon after a marriage. And, of course, both could be symptomatic of even larger forces flowing through the family arteries. These latter also differ in that they are not complete passages, but more like the openings to a passage. With marriage, death, birth, and pubescence, an individual is not simply leaving one state, but going to another that is well defined. Somehow the beginning and the end are all subsumed as part of the complete passage of six months to a year; and the new state toward which the family is headed is in some ways teleologically pulling the family through the crisis. Similarly, while the biological rites of passage all deal with loss and healing, these latter rites tend only to deal with loss. They are thus more open ended. All of this is not to say that they are not ripe times for bringing change to a family, or in some cases are not symptomatic of changes already going on in the family, but they may not be in themselves natural family phenomena with all the power for healing that those experiences contain.

DIVORCE

The rate of divorce today is becoming so high as to suggest it is reaching the level of a biological imperative. And of these latter nonbiological nodal points in life, divorce would seem to portend more family change. Several religious groups have experimented with the creation of a divorce ceremony. Since the thrust of this chapter has been that rites of passage are family events, it maybe that in many cases only the second marriage or a funeral really completes that passage. I do know of one person who sent out divorce announcements with an invitation to a party: "Mrs. _____ announces the divorce of her daughter from Mr. _____ on the steps of the Court House of _____." She said that many of her female cousins took one look at it and destroyed the card before their husbands could see it.

To bring the full power of a family rite of passage to divorce, perhaps the following perspective would be helpful: To the extent that a divorce comes about because the rite of passage of marriage did not do its work (that is, successfully bring about disengagement in the family of origin), the divorce is not likely to bring real change if the original triangles are still stuck. To the extent, on the other hand, that the divorce is a result of changes in that originally stuck situation with the family of origin, which in turn unbalanced the marriage, then the divorce is more likely to offer opportunity.

In either case, if clients who come in to work on their fears of loneliness, instability, adjustment of their children, loss of moorings, and so forth (the focus of most of the self-help books on divorce) can be focused on relationships with the family of origin instead — and they often are more motivated to do so during this period — one will have made divorce a rite of passage in the fullest sense of the term.

RETIREMENT

Retirement may have more ramifications for family life than has been realized, though therapists near military bases do not have to be told this fact. The number of divorces that occur after early military retirement is quite high. The general rule would seem to be this: Where the marriage was balanced by the mother being intensely involved with the children and the father with the service (which becomes a sort of extended family), his retirement often unbalances the relationship, particularly if he now tries to reenter the family and finds himself excluded, or seeks a replacement in the form of an extramarital relationship. This phenomenon is not limited to the military and can occur with any profession that involves the husband who is deeply in his work relationship system (lawyers, clergy, etc.). That it has far-reaching ramifications may be seen from the following tale.

A couple, both of whom were only children, and both 27 years old, came in to get married after going steady for five years. They had just made the decision and wanted the wedding in a month. Naturally I asked them what they thought moved the relationship on to marriage. Though well educated, introspective, and in no way threatened by the question, they had no idea. In poking into the family history, I could find none of the usual family changes, such as deaths, marriages, or births. Then innocently she remarked, "Well, the only thing I can say that changed is that both our fathers retired last year." Five years of going steady and they suddenly realized that they were right for one another.

One possible explanation of this is that when the fathers retired, they got closer to their wives, who inadvertently let go of their children. Or perhaps this was more true of the one who was the real holdout. In any event, theoretically this is the exact opposite of the military situation where divorce results when the wife refuses to be drawn closer to the now more available spouse and still clings to the child.

It is thus clear that retirement can have significant family ramifications, and can also be induced by family events as when a parent, after a loss (through death, divorce, or marriage), begins to wonder, "What's the point of working so hard?" and begins to change his or her sights. The so-called "leaving the nest" syndrome may be similar. Another major family ramification of retirement is the onset of senile processes. If the experience with my mother and aunt has more universal application, the following rule may be true: If, around the time any older person begins to reduce significantly his or her functioning (through retirement or an illness) there is available an overfunctioning, anxious family member who, at that moment, has no receptacle for his or her energy, the likely outcome is senility for the former.

GEOGRAPHICAL UPROOTING

Geographical uprooting can also have severe consequences, particularly to the extent that it means leaving an emotionally important house or community. What is also crucial is the extent to which it changes the balance of a marriage. For example, if it takes a wife further away from her mother, it can either free her or lead her to become more dependent. In general, it might be said that such uprooting, to the extent it takes a couple further from one spouse's extended family and closer to the other's, will shift the balance, though not necessarily always in the same direction. I have seen situations where couples move toward an area in which both extended systems reside and almost blow apart in months, despite a previously content relationship.

From the other side, I have seen more than one family in therapy stuck for months on a marital problem or a problem with a child become suddenly motivated to "resolve things" as a deadline nears so that they can get on with their new life.

Here the principle given earlier is borne out again: families in flux during a rite of passage sometimes can be more easily changed at such periods. It also suggests that the changes that accompany, and often precede, geographical uprooting or retirement may be much more powerful forces than we realize. And once again the visible change, that is, the actual retirement or the move, may be symptomatic of emotional changes in the family that had been growing toward a climax for some time.

Our culture, of course, has done little to prepare families for the emotional shock waves or retirement. Interestingly, the U.S. government, sensing the life cycle importance of retirement in recent years, has instituted a program of trial retirement, where the person can change his or her mind during the first year. But even that program may be little more helpful than are trial marriages. It is the homeostatic forces of emotional balance that count, and it is very hard to get a true reading on changes in that balance until commitment is made.

What then about new ceremonies that might help such transitions? It might be possible to create these, but they would have to be centered in the family rather than the work system or the larger community, though members of those systems could be included.

Here we come face to face with what ceremonies are all about. From an individual point of view, a ceremony can help mark a feeling of change or renewal, and perhaps make one conscious of a benchmark period in one's life cycle. But it is much more than that. Ceremonies, even today, get at processes the most ancient tribes were trying to deal with in their most primitive rites. After all, it is only when we think of a person as a member of the family that the term "life cycle" makes any sense. Otherwise we should be talking in terms of life lines.

CONCLUSIONS

I have tried to show that the notion that families are primarily passive vehicles during rites of life passage, with little influence on either the outcome of the passage or the selection of the particular rites and ceremonies, does not hold up. The traditional social science focus on different cultures' customs, aided by concentration on the individual to be passed, completely ignores the possibility that the very obvious cultural differences are really rather unimportant in themselves. They may be fun to compare, but are not nearly as crucial as the unseen family process forces wearing those very cultural disguises. Indeed, all cultures as they become more sophisticated may be participating in a great illusion - namely, that the medicine men for all their hocus-pocus have only succeeded in driving the spooks and spirits further from view, and making them harder to exorcise or control. It is the demons that now wear the masks. There is a great irony here for the function of ceremonies at rites of passage. Now the culture disguises they have been enabled to assume allow them to go slipping through, right into the next generation.

When members of a family can see through the cultural camouflage, they can maintain their gaze on the family process that contributed to a rite of passage occurring at that particular time, as well as observe how these processes are at work during the rite of passage itself. That family is in a position to influence both the effectiveness of the passage and its own emotional system.

ENDNOTES

[1] I have expanded on the notion that mature traditions already are in touch with family process in "Enriching the Lifecycle Through Creative Family Participation," Draft 40 pp., 1977. Paper written for the Committee on Family Life of the Central Conference of American Rabbis. Presented to the full Conference, Toronto, June 1978. See also section on pubescence - bar mitzva.

[2] In emotional life any situation can produce exactly opposite effects and any effect can come from totally opposite situations. An awareness of this is important in observing patterns that may superficially appear different. I tried to develop this theme more fully in "The Curvature of Emotional Space," delivered at the 14th Georgetown University Family Therapy Symposium, 1977, unpublished.

[3] I am indebted to Dr. Murray Brown for this insight as reported at a Georgetown clinical monthly meeting after the death of his father.

[4] The full expansion of this view of the pernicious effects of secrets in families is in "Secrets and Systems," delivered at the 10th Georgetown University Family Symposium, 1973. Published in Collection of Selected Papers 11 (1977), edited by Lorio and McClenathan.

[5] In another experience I had with the shifting emotional forces that take place at funerals, a woman tried to kidnap her mother after her father's death because the distance from her husband made her feel that she would mourn alone. It is described in "Family Systems Thinking and a New View of Man," CCAR Journal, 18.1 (Jan. 1971).

[6] I have developed the general notion of the interrelationship between marriage and family of origin in two papers: "The Nature of the Marital Bond," delivered at the 11th Georgetown University Family Therapy Symposium, 1974, published in Collection of Selected Papers 11 (1977), edited by Lorio and McClenathan; and "Engagement and Disengagement - Family Therapy with Couples During Courtship," delivered at the eighth Georgetown University Family Therapy Symposium, 1971, published in Collection of Symposium Papers 1 (1977), edited by Andres and Lorio.

[7] An improvisational approach to the whole life cycle that tries to show how tradition can actually be preserved through the insights of family process can be found in "Enriching The Life Cycle Through Creative Family Participation" (see note 1).

WORKS CITED

Friedman, E.H. *Generation to Generation: Family Process in Church and Synagogue*. New York: Guilford, 1985.

Chapter Five

BASIC CHRISTIAN UNDERSTANDINGS

Bernard J. Cooke

What do Christians need to know in order to become disciples? I would like to propose a theological framework structured on five fundamentals:
(1) the Church
(2) Jesus the Christ
(3) the God who saves
(4) divine/human communication
(5) authentic Christian life.

Research during the past few decades has indicated the extent to which various contexts of religious education are governed by different purposes and therefore demand varying pedagogical approaches, even at times varying content matter.[1] What is needed for a catechism class of ten-year-olds is obviously not what is required for an adult education group. But what is common to all situations of religious instruction is the goal of *understanding* what religion, specifically Christianity, is all about.[2]

Having said this, one must immediately introduce a clarification: the term "understanding" can be used quite ambiguously. One can use the word to refer to a purely informational bit of knowledge: one knows that a certain denomination explains an element of belief, for example, the human need for grace, in a particular way. Anyone, with or without religious faith, can possess this kind of understanding. Or one can, with faith in the teaching role of his or her church, accept that church's doctrinal formulations about divine grace as true. Or one can understand with some accuracy the reality to which the formulation points, that is, the gracious intervention of God in human affairs. The last instance requires, of course, a certain element of personal religious experience, grounded in faith but occurring as part of one's awareness of life.

While all three instances of understanding have their place, it is the third instance, personal understanding of the reality of God acting in human life, that is the ideal which religious education tries to achieve.[3] In such understanding, one does not simply know about God as revealed in Jesus the Christ; one knows this God.

Without retreating from the position that this personal understanding of the realities accepted in faith should be the objective of religious education, we must recognize the danger involved in this stance. The danger is that people will drift toward an uncritical, imprecise religious feeling about God; that they will be content with quite inaccurate understandings of their faith. Theoretical study of education, specifically of religious education, has in recent years stressed the inter-action of cognition, affectivity, and action and the necessary contribution of each to balanced personal development. The influence of Jean Piaget and Paulo Freire has been basic but by no means isolated.[4]

The desired goal, then, combines the two elements, experience of reality and accurate knowledge. One could refer to this as "an educated understanding" of one's faith but with the proviso that one is not necessarily referring to any sophisti-cated technical explanation. More than one sophisticated explanation is faulty, and many a simple and direct grasp of religious beliefs is accurate. Such accurate explanations, however, exist only because of some competent religious instruction that was guided, at least indirectly, by careful theological scholarship.

The purpose of the present essay is to deal with this kind of religious under-standing, to discuss five elements of down-to-earth knowledge that people need in order to deal religiously with the experienced reality of their human life. This need has long been recognized by church groups and responded to by their production of educational materials to help achieve this goal. Actually the history of such efforts goes back at least as far as Luther's catechism. My essay will limit itself to Christian congregational education, though one could speak similarly about other situations of Christian instruction or about instruction in other religions. My basic presupposition is that people need relatively few basic religious understandings; but these few must be true.

1. THE CHURCH

An essay such as the present one almost inevitably deals with Christian under-standings in propositional form. It describes the content of belief in formulated statements that rather starkly lay out the claims that Christianity has made about God, about Jesus as the Christ, and about itself as a path of human salvation. Yet we know that people's actual awareness of their Christian faith and life is not cast in such abstract and certain forms: people's understanding of Christianity and their consequent self-identification as Christian is often a mixture of piecemeal information, folk tradition, civil religion, and authentic openness to the Gospel mixed with questions and ever doubts. Formal religious education has in many cases made a substantial contribution, but the experience of being part of a Christian congregation has informally imparted the awareness of Christianity that is basically operative in most people's faith. "There is simply nothing as successful or as powerful in communicating messages as a community itself. One learns reli-gious messages through models and through memories." (Greenberg 449)

If this is so, the importance of accurate understanding about the Church is evident; and this means personal understanding of the actual congregational situa-tion of which they are a part. While some knowledge of the nature and operation of "the great church" is needed, for most people it is their local Christian community that is church for them. This is where people find themselves with other Christians who are more or less like-minded; it is a center of organizing works of ministry; it is the context for most, if not all, of their public worship; it is that with which they immediately identify when they think of themselves as "religious." At times they will be involved in activity at the synod or diocese or presbytery level, or be affected by decisions taken at that level. However, most of their experience of being Christian occurs in their congregation; and indications are that the role of the local situation will increase rather than diminish in the years ahead.

As is the case with almost everything else, Christians' view of the Church has undergone considerable change in the years since World War II. Perhaps the most publicized shift occurred in Roman Catholicism when Vatican II insisted that the Church is the entire people; but much the same awakening to the importance of the laity had begun earlier in Protestant circles.[5] This represents much more than a shift in theological emphasis and theoretical understanding; it is a basic change in Christian self-identity, a broadening of both responsibility and power. However, the responsibility will be faced and the power exercised in truly Christian fashion only if women and men understand accurately the mission of the Church in history and the kind of power that is appropriate to the pursuit of that mission.

To those whose religious practice is relatively minimal and perfunctory this provokes no questions; they are content with their once-a-week (or less frequent) contact with Christianity. But for those seriously interested in Christian disciple-ship it has led to problems. At times they find the institutional structures of the Church a burden, even an obstacle to what they feel the Church should be and do. It is such people who need to understand why the structured church is necessary, why "institutionless Christianity" is an illusory ideal; who need to grasp the deeper reality of the Church as the body of Christ; and who in a new way need to identify "the Church" as themselves.

Devoted Christians must be helped to live with the human inadequacies of church structures; but something more fundamental is at stake. The experience of being Christian should be the experience of being a disciple of Christ and, along with one's fellow Christians, the body of Christ. Clearly, people cannot have such an experience if they do not understand what these terms mean. They need not be given a complicated technical explanation—Paul used the notions in dealing with communities of relatively uneducated people. However, people do need to have some grasp of the mystery dimension of Christianity and some grasp of the way in which they as disciples of Christ form part of that mystery.

Too often "the Church" has been explained to Christians as equivalent with the official levels of the Church and as an indispensable intermediary between them and God—even though the general thrust of the sixteenth-century Reformation (and of much that preceded it) was in the opposite direction. Too many Christians have not known the vivid, life-changing, and often painful experience of consciously participating in a community of believers who, as Walter Brueggemann describes, articulate an alternative view of the world and of the living God. (13-26) What needs to be taught is that the Church is not that through which Christians pass in order to reach God, but that it is they themselves who are the context of the divine presence. The Church is the situation in which they are meant to encounter God. The reign of God is in their midst.

2. JESUS THE CHRIST

Such an approach to understanding the Christian church should make it clear that correct understanding about Jesus of Nazareth is basic to Christian faith. The only ultimately distinguishing element of Christianity as a religion is the identity and role of Jesus. If he is not what Christians claim him to be, Christianity has little right to exist. Yet a random questioning of those who consider themselves Christian would reveal amazingly diverse and vague opinions about this Jesus. All would possess some knowledge that there was a historical person who lived roughly two thousand years ago, who taught, performed works of healing, and was unjustly put to death by the combined leadership of the Jews and the Romans. Some would add that Jesus is "the son of God" but would then be unable to give any precise content to this title. Most would become even less certain of their understandings if asked about the reality of Jesus' resurrection—which, incidentally, is the central element in the original Christian kerygma. And if one asked whether Jesus still exists humanly and, if so, how and where, one would probably encounter puzzled silence.

One begins to wonder what is meant by Christianity being a faith community, that is, a sharing of belief in Jesus as Christ and Lord, when one observes this lack of common understanding as to who and what Jesus really was and is. Are people in an ordinary congregation truly sharing a common view about Jesus' identity and role in human life?

What is disturbing is not that such a cacophony of voices exists but that so little attention has been paid to it. Though biblical and theological research have for some decades been focused on Christology,[6] there is still little awareness on the congregational or catechetical level that people need to discover the real Jesus, that their present understandings need correction or at the very least augmenting. Much more than theoretical knowledge about doctrine is involved; Christian prayer and Christian discipleship should be directed to the reality of the risen Christ, not to some "imagined Jesus."

Though we have only limited ability to reach back two thousand years and recover the historical circumstances into which Jesus of Nazareth was born and with which he interacted, we do have some possibilities of appreciating how Jesus' contemporaries saw him. Despite the fact that the New Testament literature views Jesus, including his historical career, in the light of the Easter experience, we can gain some insight into what Jesus was actually like and into what he actually taught and did.[7]

Circumscribed though our accurate knowledge of the historical figure Jesus is, it contains elements that are of immense importance to Christians' down-to-earth religious beliefs. The extraordinary ordinariness of Jesus, his refusal to exercise institutionalized political power, his friendship with and concern for the marginated of society, his fidelity to the prophetical vocation that was his, his view of God as irrevocably compassionate, the unassuming dignity that was his because of his radical honesty, the passionate commitment of bettering the lives of people, that is, establishing God's new community—these are aspects of Jesus that are fundamental to one's understanding of what it seems to be Christian. Without our knowing this, there is no possibility of following Paul's admonition to "put on the mind of Christ Jesus."[8]

Christianity's understanding of Jesus is not confined, however, to knowledge about his roughly thirty-five years of earthly life. The Jesus about whom the New Testament speaks, the Jesus to whom Christian faith from its very beginnings has been directed, is the risen Christ, the Lord of glory.[9] And if there are difficulties in acquiring accurate knowledge about the historical Jesus, these difficulties are magnified when a faith community attempts to grasp the reality of the risen Jesus, the Christ. But at the very least, Christians' knowledge about and faith awareness of Jesus as the Christ in our lives should be guided by those elements of earliest Christianity's faith experience which underlie the New Testament literature.

Admittedly there are problems in interpreting those Gospel passages we refer to as "the apparitions of the risen Christ," but beneath the literary forms in which the primitive Christian faith is couched there lie certain basic beliefs that are normative for subsequent generations of believers: Jesus is alive; Jesus is humanly alive, though in some different situation of human existing; Jesus remains in relationship with those who accept Christ in faith—as a matter of fact, there is a life bond that unites Christians with Jesus; in his new fulfilled situation Jesus enters into the definitive stage of his ministry, because he can now share with others the full power of his Spirit which is his God's Spirit also.

Granted that these elements of belief do not provide a detailed insight into what "resurrection" is for Jesus, and thereafter for others also, they at least give some authentically traditional guidelines for Christians who wish to form a deepening relationship with Christ. Having to discipline their religious imagination so that it does not exceed the evidence about the risen Christ provided by mainstream Christian tradition will help condition people to resist the ultimate religious temptation, which is to think about God according to their own images and likenesses.

Unless there is careful reflection about the divine, there is no hope that Christians will be able to deal accurately with the two-thousand-year-old Christian claims about the divinity of Jesus. What does it mean to say that Jesus is God's own Son, that Jesus shares full divinity with God the Father, that Jesus is—according to the great conciliar creeds from Nicaea to Chalcedon—"consubstantial in divinity" with the transcendent God? How can Christians believe that Jesus is "a divine person," one of the Trinity, and still be monotheists?

Obviously, nothing is gained by trying to tell people in the pews about "divine processions" or "spiration," about the refinements of dogmatic language that led finally to terms like "hypo-static union," about medieval and modern theology's complicated attempts to noncontradiction in Christian teaching about divine trinity. Perhaps it would be better to lead people to some realization that there is a depth in the personhood of Jesus that somehow opens onto the divine, and that at this point our ordinary human understandings break down. Perhaps the only positive understanding we possess and can communicate is that Jesus stands in unique personal relationship to the God whose transcendence we cannot grasp but can only point to. At the very least, we should not leave people with the misconception that they understand more than they do when they refer to Jesus as "the Son of God."

3. THE GOD WHO SAVES

One who accepts the teaching of Jesus is led inescapably to the ineffable mystery of the infinite God, for it is about this God whom Jesus experienced as "Abba" that he constantly spoke. But what should Christians be told about God? A simple and very important response would be: tell them what Jesus taught about God. However, in today's world simple repetition of Jesus' teaching is not sufficient. We need to plumb that teaching to discover the implied response to the questions that modern critical thought has raised with regard to the human being's ability to deal with the existence and nature of the divine.

For a relatively small group of people it is important to reflect philosophically about our human ability to know the divine in itself. For the bulk of people in the average congregation it is more practical to assume the existence of God, to bypass sophisticated questions about the reality of God-in-self, and to concentrate on what biblical faith and Christian tradition hand on as "revelation," that is, God-for-us.

What this requires is explaining the Christian understanding of salvation. What is it that God is doing in human lives to enable men and women to reach their destiny? In our world with its absorption of the scientific mentality into even or common-sense view of the realities that surround us, the rather naive understandings of "divine providence" that prevailed in former times are no longer acceptable. Indeed, the question "What is meant by divine providence?" may be the most radical religious question facing us today. In the wake of scientific advances, the very notion of salvation is questioned; many people see secular solutions as adequate to individual and societal needs. At the same time, there is widening disillusionment with the "solutions" offered by contemporary science and technology and an obvious retreat by many to a religious and cultural fundamentalism. Again, there is a widespread challenge to Christianity's teaching about salvation that comes—at least in the affluent "first world"—from consumerism, the absorbing quest for possessing things, the promise that having the latest style and gimmick will bring happiness, the demand for instant satisfaction of "needs" that for the most part are artificially created by advertising.

Actually, an effective explanation for salvation must deal with two issues: the nature of the evil from which human beings need to be saved and the manner in which God helps human beings overcome this evil. Science's challenge has forced us to confront both these matters in a new way, but a way that promises to be truly religious. Because of modern psychological insights, we have greater clarity about the forces that work to diminish our human personhood. Because of sociological research, we understand better the institutional forms and procedures by which human beings are opposed and harmed. Drawing from such knowledge, Christian faith can now go a step farther in understanding both individual and social sin.[10]

For a number of reasons, it is of greater practical importance that people develop a more accurate understanding of sin. It is not enough to criticize the excessively negative approach to human moral behavior that for so many centuries characterized Christian discussion about son. An alternative and more balanced insight into human culpability is needed so that today's Christians can face life's responsibilities with maturity and without anxiety.[11]

On the individual level, it is important to recover some of the biblical perspective of sin as infidelity and folly and refusal to accept the dependence that is intrinsic to creaturehood. On the public level, Christians today need to regain the prophetic insight into the evil of social oppression and injustice, not only admitting that such things are evil but discovering the manner in which such evils are systematized in the institutions and embedded in the prejudices of modern societies.[12]

While the universal human experiences of suffering and death must be dealt with, and human effort must continue to be directed toward reducing suffering as far as possible, a Christian perspective cannot see either suffering or death as ultimate evil. Even for those engaged in the healing professions, death should not be viewed as defeat and its avoidance the primary objective. Evil strikes at human beings most basically when it diminishes or even destroys the personal dimension of people's lives.[13]

What Christians need is not some theoretical attempt to reconcile the existence of evil with the existence of a good God. Rather, they need to appreciate what the real evils are that threaten their humanity in today's world, what the "real sins" are that stand as barriers to people reaching their destiny; and they need to understand what concretely constitutes salvation from these evils. What, for example, can be done to save the starving people of the earth from the tragic human indignity that goes along with abject impoverishment, and what can be done to save affluent peoples from the spiritual dullness that prevents them from being bothered by the fact that their high level of economic well-being is bought at the expense of others' starvation?

In this arena of good struggling with evil, what is God's role in saving humanity? What, on the other hand, are human beings expected to do as their share in saving themselves? Obviously we are here confronted with the age-old question of faith and good works but in terms of the concrete circumstances and responsibilities of people who call themselves Christian. People need to understand what it is that God is doing in their lives if they are to cooperate with this divine action.

It is always perilous to suggest that we today have a more correct and workable understanding of Christian life than our predecessors in the faith. But it does seem that a somewhat new and more understandable approach to "grace" has come to the fore in recent theology: an approach that sees God's self-revealing presence in the consciousness of believers as a radically transforming force that is capable of saving them and through their actions saving others as well. This perspective is, of course, very biblical;[14] the New Testament writings are filled with it—for example, the application of "Emmanuel" ("God with us") to Jesus in the infancy narrative, Luke's theology of Jesus as replacement of the temple, and the prologue of John and its notion of the divine World dwelling with us. However, this biblical view needs to be translated into people's understanding of how God dwells with them in today's world, of how God's presence is meant to transform individuals and society, and of what is expected of human beings in response to God's presence.

4. DIVINE/HUMAN COMMUNICATION

A more adequate understanding of grace leads us logically to the fourth area of understanding that is needed as ground for Christians living out their faith. When one speaks of "presence," one is referring to a reality that comes into being when one person communicates with another, when somehow the "speaker" inhabits the consciousness of the "hearer." In the case of Christians dealing with the God revealed in Jesus, the open hearing of the word of God is faith. But in saying this, one must remain aware that the Word is incarnated in the risen Christ and that "hearing the word" is a matter of establishing personal friendship with Christ.[15]

For Christians to develop this kind of relationship with Christ and through Christ with God, they must have an understanding of prayer. What kind of communication can actually take place between God and human beings, and what is the risen Jesus' role in such interchange?

One thing that does have to be highlighted in explaining the nature of prayer to people is that the initiative in divine/human communication is always on the divine side. Contrary to people's ordinary view, God does not answer our prayers—at least in the way we think God does. We tend to think we turn to God in prayer and God then responds. Such a position of response would, of course, imply that we effect a change in God, something that philosophical reflection about the transcendent tells us is incompatible with divine reality. Beyond philosophy, biblical revelation insists that God takes the initiative: it is God who unexpectedly calls Moses, who does the same with the great charismatic prophets, who is described as going out to search for sinful Israel and bring about reconciliation of the people and God. The New Testament is no less explicit: God so loved the world that God sent God's own Son (John 3:16); the good shepherd goes out to seek the lost sheep (John 10); and the book of Revelation describes God standing at the door and knocking.

Very simply, God speaks first and Christian prayer is a response to that divine word. That implies, however, that people must realize how and where and when God speaks. The Bible occupies, of course, a privileged place as word of God; but the history of biblical interpretation proves that understanding what God is saying through these texts is far from obvious. While the average man or woman of faith need not be acquainted with the latest advances of scriptural research, their personal use of the Bible should be guided by responsible modern scholarship.[16] If we are to hear the Bible as God's word, it is critically important to extract meaning from the texts rather than reading our own presuppositions into them.

Beyond the scriptural word, however, there are other situations that faith sees as communication from God to humanity. Liturgical worship should function in this way; actually, it should provide the paradigmatic occasion for proclaiming, hearing, and responding to the biblical word. Both Protestantism and Catholicism are today recovering their traditions about the evangelical dimension of liturgy, something that should lead to increased experience and appreciation of liturgy as communal prayer that is also deeply personal.

Paradoxically, at a time when spiritual values are disappearing from many contexts of human life there seems to be a widening interest in prayer. However one wishes to evaluate them, the huge audiences listening to electronic preachers, the worldwide spread of the charismatic movement, the attraction to the person and thought of Thomas Merton, the fascination of so many for Eastern contemplation—all are symptoms of a desire and search for genuine personal contact with the divine. But if Christians are to pray authentically, to come into real relation with the true God, they need to be guided by those who themselves understand what it means to pray as a Christian.

Most basically, people need to understand how the happenings of their lives are truly "word of God." This does not mean that they should come to see these daily experiences as a series of "little miracles" that God is specially working for them—such a view may be pious, but it is erroneous. Rather, they need to be led to the understanding that all created existence is grounded in the divine self-giving, that human life is permeated by God's invitation to accept divine presence, and that the Spirit of God does indeed work wherever human beings are deeply concerned for one another's well-being.[17] If awareness of this pervading presence of God is nurtured, it will lead naturally to prayerful response. Indeed, the awareness is itself the most basic response.

5. AUTHENTIC CHRISTIAN LIFE

A fifth area of understanding is even more down-to-earth: What does one mean by the term "a good Christian"? There have been times when this term was applied to any morally respected person, independent really of any genuinely religious faith. More recently, particularly with renewed interest in and knowledge of the New Testament writings, we recognize that "being Christian" is more than just "being ethically good," though it obviously includes the latter. But what precisely is one expected to do in order to be "a good Christian," a follower of "the way"?

Basic to any response to this question is an understanding of "sin," guilt," and "conscience," three terms whose meaning has been seriously challenged these past few decades. Earlier in this essay we studied the way in which a more accurate insight into sin is required in order to grasp the meaning of "salvation." But a correct view of sin is needed also if Christian experience of guilt is to be honest and balanced. While there is no doubt that some past generations focused excessively on human sinfulness, to the point of creating neurotic guilt feelings in many Christians, the existence of sin is a reality of human life that must be acknowledged and maturely handled. In a "Christianity come of age" the idea of sin needs to be demythologized; but that does not say that its reality should be denied. While the full notion of sin can be appreciated only in a context of faith, the fact of human sinful activity is only too clearly evidenced in human experience.

Biblical studies have recently contributed a great deal to clarifying our understanding of sin. Sin as *alienation*, already a basic category in Old Testament thought, is not too difficult to grasp without referring directly to God. But sin as *infidelity*, though necessarily understood by reference to human relationships in which betrayal occurs, can find its full meaning only in terms of the gratuitous love of God being stupidly refused by human beings. To the person who has pondered the prophetic designation of Israel's sinfulness as "adultery," any description of sin as simply violation of laws, even God's laws, is most inadequate. More is involved than obtaining an accurate view of sin; seeing sin as infidelity to human and divine love makes it possible to move toward realistic and effective conversion for conversion consists basically in choosing to love oneself, others, and God. This does not imply that conversion is easy, but at least one knows what one has to do, which is the indispensable first step toward doing it.

Today, thanks in large part to advances in psychology, we understand better the complex dynamics that underlie people's moral behavior. We are less prone to attribute ethically deviant actions to malice or bad will, because we are conscious that social conditioning or psychological imbalance can limit some people's culpability. This is all to the good; it helps keep us from rash judgment of others and contributes to a more realistic appraisal of our own behavior. But at the same time, we need to avoid the extreme of attributing all misbehavior to psychological compulsion or environmental impact. Sin is a reality; perhaps it is not as pervasive as some earlier generations thought, but sin is still one of the key determinants in human affairs. And when persons sin, the appropriate Christian awareness—as a matter of fact, the sane response—is a sense of guilt.

Here, again, there is an area of important personal understanding with which religious education must deal. Christians must know clearly that true guilt is a conscious judgment that one has done something seriously wrong, that one has harmed oneself or other human beings, and that in so doing one has been unfaithful to the love relationship with God in Christ to which one is pledged by Christian baptism. Authentic guilt is not an anxiety-ridden guilt feeling; it is an honest and mature judgment that one has done wrong, an admission or moral failure, grounded in the resolve to do otherwise in the future.

Perhaps the best pedagogical approach to explaining the reality of "guilt" is to concentrate on people's *responsibility*. The positive knowledges and attitudes that education tries to contribute to a person's moral development have to do with grasping the ways in which one can and should respond to the challenges of life. Unless people understand accurately the responsibilities they bear as Christians, they cannot become aware of the irresponsibility they incur in shirking or refusing these responsibilities.

But should not truly Christian behavior go beyond avoidance of sin, beyond the correct social behavior expected of any person? One clear way of responding to this question is in terms of *discipleship*. A Christian should in his or her life translate the example of Jesus into actions needed in our world. However, it would be a mistake to understand "disciple of Christ" as one who *succeeds* Jesus in the ministry he carried on two millennia ago. Rather, since Christians in community are truly the body of Christ, discipleship is a matter of co-working with the risen

Christ who still is present in Spirit to the human history that Christ seeks to transform. To be a disciple of Christ, to be truly a Christian, a person must allow the direction of the Spirit to be the norm for his or her choices and actions; one must be faithful to Christ's Spirit.

No doubt about it—this approach to judging which behavior is appropriately Christian is less absolute, and for that reason less comfortable, than an approach in terms of obeying specified laws. It is not only less clear-cut; it is more demanding, for it involves the total personal response of a Christian and not just this or that particular element of behavior.

But because they are so open-ended and encompassing, the demands of discipleship need to be spelled out somewhat for people who must live in the actual circumstances of today's world. This is an element of religious education that must continue throughout the adult life of a Christian, an element that must be supplied within the context of a congregation; it will not be supplied elsewhere. Sunday sermons, adult education programs, special lecture series—all need to work together to indicate to people the practical dictates of Christian faith in our rapidly changing world.

At a time when Christian ministry has taken on a broader meaning, when in all the Churches ministerial activity is shared with a widening group of the non-ordained, there is increased need to develop people's ability to discern the Christian course of action in their professional, familial, and public life. Orthopraxis is now seen to parallel orthodoxy as a basic criterion for judging the genuineness of people's faith. This in no way detracts from the importance of correct understanding, which my essay has tried to emphasize. Any appraisal of what it means to act as "a good Christian" will be controlled by one's understanding of Jesus as the Christ, of the Church, of God's saving grace, and of Christian discipleship. Understanding of itself will not suffice. Knowledge is not virtue, but authentic Christian faith and life exist correlative to an accurate understanding of the Gospel.

END NOTES

[1] This is reflected, for example, in the theme symposia published in *Religious Education* which have dealt with special groups such as adults or adolescents. See vols. 74.3 (1979), 76.4 (1981), 80.1 (1985), and 81.2 (1986).

[2] This is not to deny that understanding is sought for the purpose of more authentic religious behavior. "Orthodpraxis" has become more prominent as a formal criterion of genuine Christian faith. But there is a commonsense recognition that people's actions are correlative to what they know. An interesting interchange on the role of cognition in religious education is provided by Charles Melchert, "'Understanding' as a Purpose of Religious Education," *Religious Education* 76 (1981): 178-86 and the response of Craig Dykstra, *Vision and Character: A Christian Educator's Alternative to Kohlberg* (New York: Paulist, 1981: 1987-94.

[3] Such religious education is quite different from the "religious studies" that are pursued in college or university. The latter are on principle confined to

description or analysis that brackets the truth claims of the religion being studied. For an indication of the extent to which the relation of such religious studies to theology or to religious education is still uncertain and debated, one could examine the presidential addresses given to the national convention of the American Academy of Religion in 1977 by Schubert Ogden, "Theology and Religious Studies: Their Difference and the Difference it Makes," *Journal of the American Academy of Religion* 46 (1978): 3-18 and in 1979 by Langdon Gilkey, "The AAR and the Anxiety of Nonbeing: An Analysis of Our Present Cultural Situation," *Journal of the American Academy of Religion* 48 (1980): 5-18.

[4] For a thorough discussion of the issue and a critical absorption of the insights of Freire and Piaget, see Thomas H. Groome, *Christian Religious Education: Sharing Our Story and Vision* (New York: Harper, 1980).

[5] See chapter 2 in the dogmatic Constitution on the Church in Austin Flannery, ed., *Vatican Council II: The Conciliar and Post Conciliar Documents*, vol. 1, new rev. ed. (Collegeville, MN: Liturgical, 1984); and section 6 of *The Evanston Report: The Second Assembly of the World Council of Churches* (New York: Harper, 1955), on the 1954 meeting of the World Council of Churches.

[6] See Bernard Cooke, "Horizons on Christology in the Seventies," Horizons 6 (1979): 193-217. Probably the most comprehensive synthesis of recent exegetical and theological research is the two-volume work of Edward Schillebeeckx, Jesus: *An Experiment in Christology* (New York: Crossroad, 1979), and *Christ: The Experience of Jesus as Lord* (New York: Crossroad, 1980). On Christology and religious education, see Reginald Fuller, "The Nature and Function of New Testament Christology," in *Emerging Issues in Religious Education*, ed. Gloria Durka and Joanmarie Smith (New York: Paulist, 1976).

[7] While textual methodologies, form, source, and redaction criticism have made a major contribution, a rich new body of insight has come with more sociological studies, such as Gerd Theissen, *Sociology of Early Palestinian Christianity* (Philadelphia: Fortress, 1978), and John G. Gager, *Kingdom and Community: The Social World of Early Christianity* (Englewood Cliffs, NJ: Prentice-Hall, 1975).

[8] In his essay "The Two Pedagogies: Discipleship and Citizenship," *Education for Citizenship and Discipleship*, ed. Mary Boys (New York: Pilgrim, 1989), John Coleman summarizes the crucial aspects of Jesus's ministry for discipleship as (1) "decisive dispositions" such as surrender to the Father, self-sacrificing love, and option for the poor; (2) "crucial paradigmatic actions: such as foot washing, healing, the cross, and forgiveness; and (3) a utopian teaching related to the reign of God" in parables, narratives, and teaching sayings. Coleman cautions, however, that discipleship is not mere imitation of Jesus' actions but a "metanormative ethic" to be applied to one's own context (pp. 45-48). See my discussion of "authentic Christian life," in this essay.

[9] This is not to accept the excessive dichotomy, made by some New Testament scholars, between "the Jesus of history" and "the Christ of faith." Several recent studies, for example, Michael Cook, *The Jesus of Faith: A Study in Christology* (New York: Paulist, 1981), have highlighted the experiential continuity of Jesus' disciples: the Jesus experienced in their Easter consciousness was the Jesus they had known during his public ministry.

[10] Both the broad and diversified development of psychology of religion and the emergence of "political theology" (including "theology of liberation") constitute major resources for religious education in this regard. For a cross-sectional view of the recent impact of study in the psychology of religion, see Peter Homans, ed., *The Dialogue Between Theology and Psychology* (Chicago: Chicago UP, 1968). An introduction to "theology of liberation" is provided by Robert McAfee Brown, *Theology in a New Key: Responding to Liberation Themes* (Philadelphia: Westminster, 1978).

[11] On the development of mature moral responsibility, see Walter Conn, *Conscience* (Birmingham: Religious Education, 1981).

[12] See, for example, Peter L. Berger, *Pyramids of Sacrifice: Political Ethics and Social Change* (New York: Basic, 1974). While they do not deal directly with ethical judgment, Richard J. Barnet and Ronald E. Muller, *Global Reach: The Power of the Multinational Corporations* (New York: Simon & Schuster, 1974), present a compelling picture of the massive institutional forces that operate to oppress millions in today's world.

[13] Interestingly, Edward Schillebeeckx in *Christ* focuses both the initial Christian "Eastern experience" and present-day application of that experience on the phenomenon of human suffering and on the salvation from suffering which Christianity is meant to implement.

[14] See Samuel Terrien, *The Elusive Presence: Toward a New Biblical Theology* (San Francisco: Harper, 1978).

[15] Probably no contemporary thinker has provided more profound insight into the notion of hearing the word of God than has Karl Rahner, particularly in his *Hearers of the Word* (New York: Herder, 1969).

[16] See Mary C. Boys, "Religious Education and Contemporary Biblical Scholarship," *Religious Education* 74 (1979): 182-97. She points out the benefits of modern biblical studies but urges a closer working relationship between religious education and scholarly research.

[17] One of the most important present-day developments along this line is feminist theological reflection upon women's experience. See, for example, the American Academy of Religion 1981 presidential address of Jill Raitt, "Strictures and Structures: Relational Theology and a Woman's Contribution to Theological Conversation," *Journal of the American Academy of Religion* 50 (1982): 3-17.

WORKS CITED

Brueggemann, Walter. "The Legitimacy of a Sectarian Hermeneutic: 2 Kings 18-ff19." *Education for Citizenship and Discipleship.* Ed. Mary Boys. New York: Pilgrim, 1989.

Greenberg, Irving. "From Modernity to Post-Modernity: Community and the Revitalization of Traditional Religion." *Religious Education* 73 (1978): 449-69.

Chapter Six

FAITH DEVELOPMENT THROUGH THE FAMILY LIFE CYCLE

James W. Fowler, Ph. D.

INTRODUCTION

We begin our journeys of selfhood and faith development in families. In recent years, much attention has been given to the dynamics of individual growth in faith.[1] Yet, families, too, have their life cycles. Family systems develop, grow, and meet predictable crises or turning points. This essay will show the interrelation of family dynamics and faith development as seen through the complementary lenses of faith development theory, family life-cycle perspectives, and family systems descriptions. The concluding section will offer some thoughts on positive and practical directions for the Church's ministry to and with families.

Before turning to the study of families *per se* we need to inquire into the dynamics of faith. First, I will invite you to consider faith as a human universal—a core dimension of our personal and collective lives and a central aspect of our nature as meaning-makers and meaning-sharers. Then we will look at Christian faith—the conversion and formation of human faith in and through relationship to God as mediated through Jesus Christ, the scriptures and teachings of the Church, and the ongoing illumination of the Holy Spirit.

FAITH AND CHRISTIAN FAITH

Let us begin by considering faith as a dynamic and generic human experience. I make the assumption that, as human beings, we are created with capacities and the need for faith from the beginning. Whether or not we are explicitly nurtured in faith in religious or Christian ways, we are engaged in forming relationships of trust and loyalty to others. We shape commitments to *causes* and *centers of value*. We form allegiances and alliances with *images and realities of power*. We form and shape our lives in relationship to master stories. In these ways, we join with others in the finding and making of meaning. All of us are engaged in the dynamics of faith.

First, faith is a dynamic pattern of personal trust in and loyalty to a *center* or to *centers of value*. What do I mean by this term "center of value?" We rest our hearts, we focus our life, in persons, in causes, in ideals, or institutions that have supreme worth to us. We attach our affections to those persons, institutions, causes or things that promise to give worth and meaning to our lives. A center of value in your life or mine is something which calls forth love and devotion. It therefore exerts ordering power on the rest of our lives and our attachments.

Family can be one such profound center of value. Success and one's career can be important centers of value. One's nation or an ideological creed can be of life-centering importance. Money, power, influence, and sexuality can all be idolatrous centers of value in our lives. For some persons and groups, religious institutions constitute dominant centers of value. All of these and many more can be centers of value in our lives. Of course, God is meant to be the supreme value in our lives.

Second, faith is trust in and loyalty to *images* and *realities of power*. You and I are finite creatures. We live in a dangerous world. We and those whom we love are vulnerable to arbitrary power and destruction in this world. In such a world, how do we align ourselves so as to feel sustained in life and in death? "The Lord is my Shepherd, I shall not want." That is a statement about alignment with power and the placing of our reliance on security. You could also say, "My stock-portfolio is my shepherd, I shall not want." Or we could say, nationally speaking, "The Star Wars missile defense system is our shepherd, we shall not want." Where we align ourselves with power to sustain us in life and death is an important faith question.

Third, faith is trust in and loyalty to *shared master stories or core stories*. In the 1960s, Eric Berne emerged with his approach called transactional analysis. One of the key ideas in transactional analysis was the notion of a *script*—a kind of unconscious story that takes form in us before we are five years of age and which, in a sense, shapes and guides unconsciously the choices and decisions that we make as we move along our lives. A core story is a little like that. It often begins unconsciously and gradually. We make it more conscious and explicit as something we are committed to. A friend of mine studied prisoners in a federal prison some years ago. He found, among those who had tattoos, that 60% had chosen some variant of the phrase "born to lose," a master story engraved into their skin.

> Faith is covenantal or triadic in structure. We are not solitary in our faith. Faith involves trust in and loyalty to other persons. That trust and loyalty with others is confirmed and deepened by our shared trust and loyalties to centers of value, images of power, and stories that transcend us as individuals and bind us together. This is what we mean by covenant. Covenant is trust and loyalty, commitment between persons and within groups that is ratified and deepened by a shared trust in and loyalty to something, someone, Reality, God, or some set of values that transcends us. Faith always has this triadic, this covenantal structure.

Understood generically as a human universal, faith includes but is not limited to or identical with religion. You can have faith that is not religious faith. Common examples include communism, materialism, or what some fundamentalists call "secular humanism." As a cumulative tradition, a religion is made up of expressions of the faith of people in the past. It can include scriptures and theology, ethical teachings and prayers, architecture and music, art and patterns of teaching and preaching. In this sense, religion gives forms and patterns for the shaping of the faith of present and future persons. Religions are the cumulative traditions that we inherit in all their varieties and forms. Religious faith, on the other hand, is the personal appropriation of relationship to God through and by means of a religious tradition.

Just as we can distinguish faith from religion, it is also important to clarify the relation between faith and *belief*. Belief is one of the important ways of expressing and communicating faith. But belief and faith are not the same thing, particularly in this modern period. Since the Enlightenment of the 18th century, many people have come to understand belief as intellectual assent to propositions of dubious verifiability. As Mark Twain put it, "Faith is believing what any damn fool knows ain't so."

Faith is deeper than belief. Hopefully, our beliefs are congruent with and expressive of our faith. But faith is deeper and involves unconscious motivations as well as those that we can make conscious in our belief and in our actions.

How should we talk about Christian faith? I propose that we see Christian faith as a conversion, a forming or re-forming of human faith. Christian faith is a dynamic pattern of personal trust in and loyalty to:

* God as the source and creator of all value, as disclosed and mediated in Jesus Christ, and through the Church, as inspired by the Holy Spirit. As such Christian faith is *Trinitarian* faith.
* The actual and coming reign of God as the hope and power of the future, and as intending justice and love among human kind. In this sense Christian faith gives us a horizon and vision, a horizon of hope grounded in a trust in the actual, present and coming reign of God.
* God, in Christ, as the Loving, Personal Redeemer and Reconciler calling us to repent and freeing us from the bondage of Sin. Christ frees us from anxiety about death, from the threat of separation from love, and from our hostility and alienation from each other.
* The Church, as body of Christ, as visible and invisible extension of the ministry and mission of Christ.

Faith development in terms of Catholic Christian faith involves a dynamic interplay of human faith and Christian faith and the gradual and ongoing process of conversion of our human faith in the direction of Christian faith. Our story becomes re-shaped by the Christian story. Our reliance on power comes to center on our hope in the Kingdom of God. Our valuing comes to center in the love of God who is the source, center, and creator of all that has value and worth. We become contemporary instances or incarnations of the Christian story.

STAGES OF FAITH — A BRIEF OVERVIEW

To orient ourselves to the dynamics of development in faith, let us consider an abbreviated description of seven stages of faith found and refined across more than fifteen years of research.[2]

Primal Faith. We all start as infants. A lot that is important for our lives of faith occurs *in utero*, and then in the very first months of our lives. We describe the form of faith that begins in infancy as Primal Faith. This first stage is a pre-language disposition, a total emotional orientation of trust off-setting mistrust, which takes form in the mutuality of one's relationships with parents and others. This enables us to overcome or offset the anxiety resulting from separations which occur during infant development. Piaget has helped us understand infant development as a succession of cognitive and emotional separations toward individuation from those who provide initial care. Earliest faith is what enables us to undergo these separations without undue experiences of anxiety or the fear of the loss itself. One can readily see how important the family is in the nurturing and incubation of this first Primal stage of faith.[3]

Intuitive-Projective Faith. This is a style of faith that emerges in early childhood with the acquisition of language. Here imagination, stimulated by stories, gestures, and symbols, and not yet controlled by logical thinking, combines with perception and feelings to create long-lasting faith images. These images represent both the protective and threatening powers surrounding one's life. If we are able to remember this period of our lives, we have some sense of how important, positively and negatively, it is in the formation of our life-long orientations in faith. When conversion occurs at a later stage in one's life, the images formed in this stage have to be re-worked in some important ways.

Mythic-Literal Faith. This emerges in the childhood elementary school years and beyond. Here the developing ability to think logically, through concrete operational thinking, helps one to order the world with categories of causality, space, time, and number. This means we can sort out the real from make-believe, the actual from fantasy. We enter into the perspectives of others. We become capable of capturing life and meanings in narrative and stories.

Synthetic-Conventional Faith. This stage characteristically begins to take form in early adolescence. Here new cognitive abilities make possible mutual, interpersonal perspective-taking. We begin to see ourselves as others see us. We begin to construct the *interiority* of ourselves and others. A new step toward interpersonal intimacy and relationship emerges. A personal and largely unreflective synthesis of beliefs and values evolves to support identity and to unite one in emotional solidarity with others. This is a very important stage of faith, one which can continue well into adulthood and throughout a person's life.

Individuative-Reflective Faith. With young adulthood or beyond, the stage we call Individuative-Reflective Faith appears. One begins to critically reflect on the beliefs and values formed in previous stages. In this stage, persons begin to rely upon third person perspective-taking. This means constructing a perspective that is neither just that of the self or reliant upon others, but is somehow above them both—a transcendental ego, if you will. The third person perspective brings objectivity and enables us to understand the self and others as part of a social system. Here we begin to see the internalization of authority, the development of an executive ego. This stage brings a new quality of responsibility for the self and for one's choices. It marks the assumption of the responsibility for making explicit choices of ideology and lifestyle. These open the way for more critically self-aware commitments in relationships and in vocation.[4]

Conjunctive Faith. At Mid-Life or beyond, frequently, we see the emergence of Conjunctive Faith. This stage involves the embrace and integration of opposites, or polarities, in one's life. Now what does this abstract language mean? It means realizing, in mid-life, that one is both young and old, that young-ness and old-ness are held together in the same life. It means recognizing that we are both masculine and feminine, with all of the meanings those characterizations have. It means coming to terms with the fact that we are both constructive people and, inadvertently, destructive people. St. Paul captured this in Romans 7. He said, "The good I would do I do not do, the evil I would not do I find myself doing. Who will save me from this body of death?"

There are religious dimensions to the reintegration of polarities in our lives. Mary Sharon Reilly, a Cenacle sister who specializes in spiritual direction for people at mid-life, titled a paper she has written on her work, "Ministry to Messiness." This messiness has to do with the holding together of polarities in midlife existences.

In the Conjunctive stage, symbol and story, metaphor and myth, both from our own traditions and from others, seem to be newly appreciated, in what Paul Ricoeur has called a second or a willed naivete. Having looked critically at traditions and translated their meanings into conceptual understandings, one experiences a hunger for a deeper relationship to the reality that symbols mediate. In that deeper relationship, we learn again to let symbols have the initiative with us. The *Spiritual Exercises of St. Ignatius* have been for me the most important single source of learning how to submit to the reality mediated by Christian symbols and story. It is immensely important to let biblical narrative draw us into it and let it read our lives, reforming and reshaping, rather than our reading and forming the meanings of the text. This marks a second naivete as a means of entering into those symbols.

Universalizing Faith. Beyond paradox and polarities, persons in this stage are grounded in a oneness with the power of being or God. Their visions and commitments seem to free them for a passionate yet detached spending of the self in love, devoted to overcoming division, oppression and violence, and in effective anticipatory response to an inbreaking commonwealth of love and justice, the reality of an inbreaking Kingdom of God.

FAMILIES: COVENANT COMMUNITIES OF BECOMING IN SELFHOOD AND FAITH

Let us begin by considering families in relation to God's covenant creativity. Herbert Anderson has written a very useful book on families and pastoral care. (Anderson 1984) He identifies three major functions in God's purposes for families. As part of God's co-creation or our co-creation with God, *procreation* is a basic task and calling of family life. Similarly, families contribute to social stability by the process of *socialization*. This means teaching norms, values and rules; forming habits and attitudes in relation to stories and orientations; teaching behaviors and skills, and the like. In the third place, families contribute to the possibility of people becoming *unique individuals before God*. As Johannes Metz would say, our families are the context where we first begin the journey toward becoming "subjects before God" — agents in our own history and responsible selves, as it were.

Families, then, are an essential part of God's covenant creativity. I would like to press this point further by saying that the family is where we first construct our sense of *ontological reality*. *Ontos* is the Greek word for being; ontology is the science that studies the structuring of being. I am saying in a very existential and personal way, the family is the context in which we first construct our sense of what reality as a whole is like. In family, we construct our first practical ontology. That's what makes families so crucially important for the formation of faith.

In families, we participate in our first social constructions of reality. We form our deep feelings regarding what can be counted upon or what can be depended upon in our primary relationships. We participate in the forming of a first sense of *identity*—who I am, who I can become, what I am worth or not worth. In the family, we have our first and most formative experiences of fundamental attachments. This is very abstract language for referring to our first love relationships and to relationships in which we participate with loyalty and care. In families, we have our first experiences with what we may call "proto-typical rituals." The changing of diapers can become a proto-typical ritual. Feeding a baby can be a proto-typical ritual. Bed-time with prayers and other kinds of saying good-night are proto-typical rituals. In these ways we order our lives so as to give and receive care. Such rituals are sacramental, just as much as what happens at the altar or anywhere else. They convey a sense of love, grace, worth, and meaning to life.

Moreover, in the family, we have our first experiences of the dynamics of intimacy and of conflict. Conflict is essential to growth and strength. The question is how to make conflict growthful in a context of love and reconciliation, rather than letting it become merely destructive and alienating.

The family, in its myriad forms, meets four clusters of ontic needs, that is needs that are essential for being and well-being. In our families, we learn to *belong* and to experience *being irreplaceable*. On the little stage of the family, where it is safe, we try our first experiences of *autonomy* and *agency*. These two sets of needs balance each other: Belonging and being separate—being *a part*, and being *apart from*. And then there's our first and most formative experiences of participation in *shared meanings* and *rituals*. Finally, the family provides for *bodily well-being*, for nurture, wellness, and care. It provides opportunities for sexual identification through sustained opportunities to relate to people of the same and opposite sex, and to learn something about the meaning of our gender.

Families represent networks of implicit and explicit covenants. In *The Hurried Child*, David Elkind helps us to see that one of the important elements of early socialization for children is learning the family's covenant system. The covenant system, only partly explicit, determines what freedoms will be given children and what responsibilities will be expected from them. It determines what achievements are expected and what support can be counted on. The covenant system stipulates what loyalty will be expected or required from family members, and what commitment will be given by those who require it. This is a crucially important part of pre-school socialization. It has to be reworked and renegotiated as we move through each of the stages of the personal and family life-cycle. (Elkind 120)

THE FAMILY LIFE CYCLE:
INTERLIVING STATES OF SELFHOOD AND FAITH

Many readers will already be familiar with psychosocial theories of ego development or of individual life-cycle development. The work of Erik Erikson, and a host of theorists who have come after him, taught us to think in terms of ages and stages in the life cycle.[5] These perspectives have entered our language and thought. They have become part of our shared assumptive reality.

Chart 1 (see page 106) presents Erikson's eight ages of the life cycle and Daniel Levinson's influential articulation of adult stages in psychosocial development. They are correlated here with some of the work of Anita Spencer in her 1982 book on women's adult psychological development, *Seasons: Women's Search for Self through Life's Stages.*

We will not present the positions of such psychologists in detail here. In giving this overview, I simply want to point out that with the psychosocial theories of Erikson, Levinson, Spencer and the resources she draws upon, we already have in hand some significant steps toward conceptualizing the family life-cycle. These theorists not only look at the individual ego in evolution, but they look at the self in its biological development and in its social relations—in its relationships to family, to social institutions, and to the cultural images and understandings which influence it.

Nonetheless, it requires a significant conceptual step to move from theories of individual growth to a full-fledged perspective on the life cycle of families taken as units. Some of the additional complexity of looking at the family life cycle can be seen in Chart 2 (see page 107), *The Family Life Spiral.*

Chart 2, Family Life Spiral, prepared by Lee Combrinck-Graham, represents an effort to show development of the family system as a three-generational enterprise. (Combrinck-Graham 38) As we look at family systems, we must try to see at least three generations inter-living and inter-acting. As you look at Chart 2, you see that birth in a new generation corresponds with child-bearing in the parent generation and with grand-parenthood in the eldest generation. If you look at the middle years of childhood, you see a settling down—roughly the period of the thirties for the parents; then you see grandparents planning for retirement. In adolescence, you see parents dealing with mid-life transition—a 40s re-evaluation—and you see grandparents dealing with retirement. Then, as that child we've been following comes to the level of being an unattached adult, ready for marriage and courtship, we see parents dealing with issues of middle-adulthood and with renegotiating their marriage relationship. The grandparents, at this point, begin dealing with dependency and late-adulthood.

Combrinck-Graham points out that there are times of centripetal pulling together in family life-cycles. In such times the family, across generations, draws more tightly together. It seems to feel that being an intergenerational unit is the most important thing. New births and the period of early childhood constitute such centripetal periods. As we move toward adolescence, we see a more centrifugal, outward-going movement. With the launching of the young-adult children the

Chart 1 — Tentative Images of the Adult Life Cycle, Men and Women

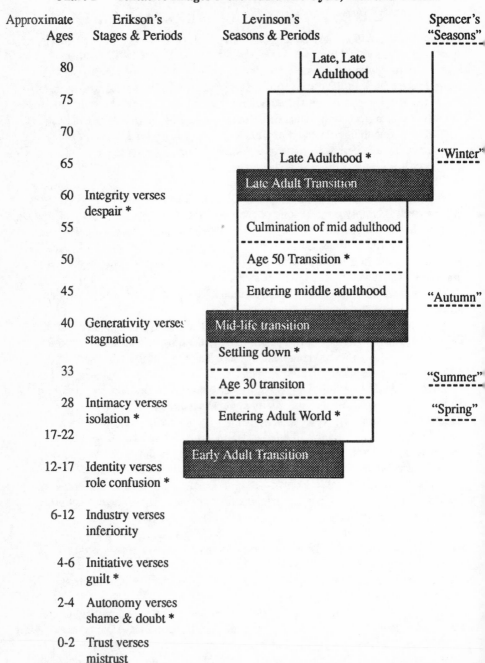

Approximate Ages	Erikson's Stages & Periods	Levinson's Seasons & Periods	Spencer's "Seasons"
80		Late, Late Adulthood	
75			
70			
65		Late Adulthood *	"Winter"
		Late Adult Transition	
60	Integrity verses despair *		
55		Culmination of mid adulthood	
50		Age 50 Transition *	
45		Entering middle adulthood	"Autumn"
40	Generativity verses stagnation	Mid-life transition	
		Settling down *	
33		Age 30 transiton	"Summer"
28	Intimacy verses isolation *	Entering Adult World *	"Spring"
17-22			
		Early Adult Transition	
12-17	Identity verses role confusion *		
6-12	Industry verses inferiority		
4-6	Initiative verses guilt *		
2-4	Autonomy verses shame & doubt *		
0-2	Trust verses mistrust		

* Indicates points where significant differences in men's and women's experiences, and in the sequencing of challenges, seem to occur.

Chart 2 — The Family Life Spiral

Family Life Spiral

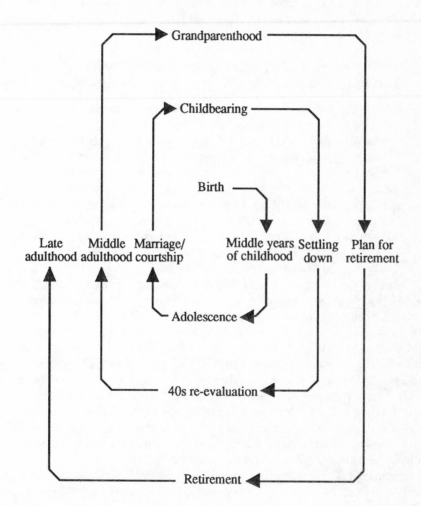

centrifugality—the spread—is at its maximum. This movement back and forth, from centripetal to centrifugal vectors, in extended family life is an important dynamic to keep in mind.

It is time to look at the stages of family life cycles and the particular tasks and challenges that come with each stage. Chart 3 (see pages 106-107) shows six stages. It is from the valuable book of Carter and McGoldrick, *The Changing Family Life Cycle*. (Carter and McGoldrick 15) (See Chapter 3 in this volume for a complete description of the family life cycle.)

IMPLICATIONS OF THE SIX STAGES
OF THE FAMILY LIFE CYCLE FOR FAITH DEVELOPMENT

(1) **Between Families**. This perspective on the family life cycle begins with the unattached young adult, one who has come through the process of formation in the family, is at an optimal centrifugal time and distance from the core of the family, and is ready for a new set of commitments and relationships. Stage One centers on the unattached young adult. The emotional process here involves accepting parent and offspring separation, the differentiation of the nearly adult child from the parents, and the claiming of one's own autonomy and self responsibility. The second order changes of this first stage involve a differentiation of self in relation to family of origin, the development of intimate peer relationships, and the establishment of the self in work or career and beginning a way of making a living.

Here the big issue that we can minister to is the shaping of vocation. Walter Brueggemann, in an article on vocation, characterizes it as "finding a purpose for one's life that is part of the purposes of God." (Brueggemann 115-129) Today, all kinds of voices shriek in the ears of young adults telling them which careers are growing and expanding, which ones are saturated, which fields they ought not to go into, which fields they ought to go into. They feel under a lot of pressure not so much to be independently wealthy, the goal of the last generation, but to be financially independent and viable at all. There is a pervading fear of downward mobility, that there will not be enough well-paying jobs. In this kind of context it is very important for churches ministering to young adults to affirm that God is calling them to places of service and fulfillment, and to communicate trust that if one is responsive to God's call there will be a way to make it economically.

In terms of faith development, the young adult would ideally be involved in transition from the Synthetic-Conventional to the Individuative-Reflective Stage of Faith. This transition can take from 5 to 7 years; it is a long transition. Care for young adults ought to nurture them in that gradual process of claiming autonomy. I am struck by how young adults in their 20s oscillate between times of claiming autonomy, and self responsibility, and times when they need the reinforcement of a conventional community of support. That oscillation is one we ought to care about.

(2) **Joining of Families through Marriage**. The second family life cycle stage focuses on newly married couples. This represents the forming of a new nuclear family and is the joining of the two nuclear and extended families of

origin, an extraordinary thing for human beings in any culture. What is the emotional process here? A commitment to the new extended family system, plus the building of and commitment to a new marital relationship. This means learning to share a home, creating rituals and order in that space, working out the regulation of eating, sleeping, sex, work, and worship. Then, there is the realignment of relationships with extended families and friends to include the spouse.

The ideal, in terms of faith development, in this second stage, involves seeing marriage as Covenant with God, with each other, with the extended families, and with the world, as an expression of individual and shared vocation. This corresponds to the continuation of the transition from the Synthetic-Conventional to the Individuative-Reflective stage of faith. In self-aware ways, the couple takes on the task of integrating new roles, new relationships and new responsibilities.

(3) **The Family with Young Children.** In the third stage of the family life cycle, new members are accepted into the family system by birth or adoption. The marital system has to be adjusted to make space for children. Young adults, or adults at whatever age, must take on parenting roles. There is also a realignment of relationships with extended family to include parenting and grandparenting roles. All three generations experience significant changes when this occurs.

We are dealing with procreation as a call to "co-creation." As part of our partnership with God, parenting brings the great opportunity and adventure of nurturing the awakening and forming of faith in our children through experience, through story, through teaching and example, and through affiliation with the community of faith. Frequently, in our time, parents feel a fair amount of vagueness about the kind of faith that they want to nurture in their children. Values are more clear: they know they want their children to go to college; they know they want them to be economically viable; they want them to be happy. But the character of Christian faith, the content, and the means to communicate that faith are not that clear. This is a crucial ministry opportunity for churches.

The effort to grow in clarity about the nurture of faith fits with parents becoming clearer about their own Christian commitments in Individuative-Reflective faith. This is crucial while their children are forming and expanding faith commitments through the Primal, Intuitive-Projective and Mythic-Literal Stages. During these important years, we see children introduced to sacraments and liturgy. This is part of the gifting of their minds and hearts with images by which they can grow. It is a great thing in the Roman Catholic tradition that there is a Mass with all of the richness of sensuous communication and kinesthetic experience it provides. Baptized children can have access to the Eucharist as early as they want to go. They later can learn the meaning of what they've experienced. To have those experiences, as part of the Christian community, is vitally important though.

Families form children's faith by involving them in formal and informal prayer. Family belonging helps to shape the *conscience of membership*—the family's covenant system and to acquire the skills to be a loyal and effective member of the family community. There they also learn the foundations of the *conscience of sacri-*

Chart 3a
The Stages of the Family Life Cycle

Family Life Cycle Stage	Emotional Process of Transition: Key Principles
1. Leaving home: Single young adults	Accepting emotional and financial responsibility for self
2. The joining of families through marriage: The new couple	Commitment to new system
3. Families with young children	Accepting new members into the system
4. Families with adolescents	Increasing flexibility of family boundaries to include children's independence and grandparents' frailties
5. Launching children and moving on	Accepting a multitude of exits from and entries into the family system
6. Families in later life	Accepting the shifting of generational roles

fice, which means learning about rules and role expectations, promise-keeping, and truth-telling. In families, children experience the awakening and formation of the voice of the *conscience of craft*—the commitment to do things "right," which may be the most fundamental voice of conscience.[6] Grandparents can be influential linkages with tradition, both family traditions and church traditions, as well as confirm-

Chart 3b
The Stages of the Family Life Cycle

Second-Order Changes in Family Status Required to Proceed Developmentally

a. Differentiation of self in relation to family of origin
b. Development of intimate peer relationships
c. Establishment of self in work and financial independence.

a. Formation of marital system
b. Realignment of relationships with extended families and friends to include spouse

a. Adjusting marital system to make space for child(ren)
b. Joining in childrearing, financial, and household tasks
c. Realignment of relationships with extended family to included parenting and grandparenting roles

a. Shifting of parent-child relationships to permit adolescents to move in and out of the system
b. Refocus on mid-life marital and career issues
c. Beginning shift toward joint caring for older generation

a. Renegotiation of marital system as a dyad
b. Development of adult-to-adult relationships between grown children and their parents
c. Realignment of relationships to include in-laws and grandchildren
d. Dealing with disabilities and death of parents (grandparents)

a. Maintaining own and/or couple functioning and interests in face of physiological decline; exploration of new familial and social role options
b. Support for a more central role of middle generation.
c. Making room in the system for the wisdom and experience of the elderly, supporting the older generation without overfunctioning for them
d. Dealing with loss of spouse, siblings, and other peers and preparation for own death; life review and integration

ers of the worth and unique calling of children in this stage.

   (4) The Family with Adolescents. With this fourth stage, the emotional process centers on development of increasing flexibility in family boundaries to include children's emerging independence. The capacities of a family to balance control and mutual trust get tested in profound ways in this stage. One of the most important gifts our children can give us at this stage is to bring us to the critical point where we learn two truths: a) We can no longer *control* them, and b) We don't have to. If they have learned the family covenantal system, if it has operated consistently and clearly, they can be trusted. In the shifting of parent-child relationships adolescents are permitted greater freedom to move in and out of the system. This shifting is made more complex by the fact that parents are refocusing their relationship on mid-life marital and career issues. A friend recently published a book called *The 5 Divorces of A Healthy Marriage*. (Straughn 1986) The book highlights the need to renegotiate and rework our marriages at different stages in the family life cycle.

Youth and parents deal with the paradox of both belonging and differentiating. Youth form identities derived from family and its commitments, as well as from the separate roles and relationships with which they experiment beyond the family in the world of peers, public, school, work, and church. Parents' ability to relinquish control depends upon their trust: a) In the loyalty of adolescents to the transcending values and standards which have shaped the family, and b) In the adolescents' judgment and initiative in particularizing or modifying the expressions of those loyalties. In how they appropriate and live out family values, adolescents teach the parent generation something, if the parent generation is willing to learn. When this is acknowledged it is a very important moment in the psycho-social development of the family. Grandparents can be important guarantors and recognizers of adolescents as successful variants of the family's patterns and loyalties. Sometimes grandparents have enough detachment to confirm grandchildren's experimental efforts to shape identity, which parents, obsessed and worried, can't confirm. Grandparents sometimes recognize the adolescent and can comfort or reassure parents about what they see.

In terms of intergenerational faith development, the ideal here is that parents are involved in transition from the Individuative-Reflective to the Conjunctive Stage of faith as they make a transition to mid-life. This would mean a truer and deeper kind of "Individuation" for the parents. Here I draw on Carl Jung's work. This kind of individuation is less tied to trying to fulfill scripts from societal or family of origin sources, but more expressive of deeper self and deeper responsiveness to God. (Whitmont; Brennan and Brewi) The parents' emerging Conjunctive faith allows space and encouragement for the more conscious and selective shaping of faith and identity going on in their adolescent children.

Confirmation for adolescents, especially as the culmination of the *Rite of Christian Initiation for Adults* as adapted for adolescents, can provide steps forward in more personal forms of prayer, more reflective entering into liturgy and sacrament, thus linking youth with personal feelings and meanings. Confirmation affirms the promise of new identity, personhood, and faith taking form in adolescents. It publicly expresses confidence in the persons they are becoming.

(5) **Launching Children and Moving On.** The central emotional process of the fifth stage of the family life cycle involves acceptance of a multitude of exits from and entries into the family system, as well as the entries into the family system of the current boyfriend, girlfriend, fiancee, and potential spouse.

Eventually, these exits necessitate a renegotiation of the marital system as a dyad. We refer to this often as the empty-nest. Renewing the marital dyad becomes a matter of great importance at this stage of the family life cycle. The joys of this stage can be the development of adult to adult relationships and friendship between grown children and their parents. This period also brings, for the parent generation, the realignment of relationships to include in-laws and grandchildren. Frequently all this is made more complex by the need to deal with disabilities and death of parents (the grandparent generation).

Here again we come to the point where the cycle begins: "Unattached Young Adults" — shaping vocation, differentiating from their families of origin, while their parents deal with reconfiguring vocation, identity, and spousal relationships at midlife. Grandparents, now in retirement, address issues of later adulthood and some dimensions of increasing dependence. The ideal here, in terms of intergenerational faith development, is that young adults would be in transition from the Synthetic-Conventional to the Individuative-Reflective stage of faith. Parents would be consolidating a Conjunctive stage. Grandparents would be manifesting the fruits of their sustained faith across their life-cycles.

(6) **The Final Stage: The Family in Later Life.** Parents have sponsored the joining of families through marriage and, perhaps, eventually have entered the more objective nurturing role of grandparents, with its mediating and enlivening of faith and family traditions. Approaching this final phase involves planning for retirement, with its reconfigurations of identity, vocation, and spousal relationships. The loss of peers and siblings must be dealt with, and, in time, one or the other of the spouses. In terms of faith development, the ideal would be to live more deeply into that quality of radical trust in God which enables a relinquishing of the need to control institutions and others. There is the need for a confirmation of identity and vocation in God. One of the important reasons for not identifying vocation exclusively with work is that the retired have incredible vocational opportunities. As a retired person, how does one find purpose for one's life that is part of the purpose of God? The lives of some elders yield evidence of transition toward Universalizing faith, with its vision and trust—and its witness—of God reigning.

We have reviewed a model which presents the inter-generational family life cycle in *ideal typical* form. In this model, there are about 20-25 years between generations. It assumes that both spouses are in relationship and that there is an on-going, orderly process to family development and growth. We all know that reality deviates from such a model in many ways. In the following, I have simply listed some of the ways in which the reality of families to which we are ministering—and in which we are living—differs from this sort of ideal model. To address adequately today's variety of family life-cycles we must include:

* Single adults, never married.
* Single adults, previously married.
* Single parents, by death, divorce, or default.
* Remarried adults, without children.
* Remarried adults with children from one or two (or more) previous families.

Blending and extending families.
* Gay or lesbian adults: single, heterosexual marriage, long-term committed same-sex relations.
* Celibate adults by calling and by choice.

In view of all this diversity, how shall we define the family? Herbert Anderson gives what I find to be a helpful definition. Family is

> A kinship system of two or more persons which involves commitment to one another over time. Kinship is achieved by marriage, birth, or adoption. Because family structure is linked to family purpose, it is necessary that the family be defined in such a way that its purposes of procreation, social stability, and individuation might be fulfilled. (Anderson 73)

The tendency to want to define persons as family who are not related by kinship can be handled in a way that respects the power and importance of such groups, yet distinguishes them from families. Anderson achieves this by using the term household. This is another term that has biblical rootage and reference. Household may provide a useful metaphor for designating stable and committed nonkinship communities that have tremendous power, influence, and support in people's lives.

FAITH DEVELOPMENT THEORY
AND STYLES OF FAMILY SYSTEMS

We come now to a part of this chapter that tries to do something essentially new. Though I have written earlier about faith development and the family, there is nothing available that tries to relate faith development theory to family systems theory. (Fowler, *Perkins Journal*) I found the clue that enabled me to make a start on this in the early part of Edward H. Friedman's book, *Generation to Generation*. There he introduces a concept developed by his teacher, Murray Bowen, M.D., who taught at Georgetown University. Bowen offered a model for characterizing the dynamics of a family system which he calls the "Scale of Differentiation." Let me quote Friedman's discussion of the meaning of differentiation:

> Differentiation means the capacity of a family member to define his or her own life's goals and values apart from surrounding togetherness pressures, to say "I" when others are demanding "you" and "we." It includes the capacity to maintain a (relatively) nonanxious presence in the midst of anxious systems, to take maximum responsibility for one's own destiny and emotional being. It can be measured somewhat by the breadth of one's repertoire of responses when confronted with crisis... Differentiation means the capacity to be an "I" while remaining connected. (Friedman 27)

What is this "Scale of Differentiation?" Bowen is fairly vague about it but very suggestive. In chart 4 we see the continuum with which he is working. On the scale from 0 to 100 we get increasing degrees of differentiation in a marital relation or a family system. At the upper end of the scale (A and B) there is a relation of optimal differentiation in which family members are able to both belong and be connected, but also to function as autonomous and self-responsible adults. Says Friedman, "There would be a maximum of "I" statements defining position, rather than blaming, "you" statements that hold the other responsible for their own condition or destiny." (28) Bowen candidly acknowledges that the most differentiated of family systems attains at best about 70% on this scale. Friedman, more bluntly, says that at least one out of every three times members of even the most differentiated family systems will get "hooked" emotionally and will respond in undifferentiated, rigid, and non-rational ways.

At the opposite end of the scale (A' and B') partners are fused or stuck together with a minimum of differentiation. Like Siamese twins, whatever either partner does automatically moves the other. Friedman writes, "There is not thinking of self, only *we* and *us* and the blaming you. The nature of the relationship might appear close. They might appear to be together, but they are really stuck together. They will wind up either perpetually in conflict, because they are so reactive to one another, or they will have a homey togetherness achieved through the total sacrifice of their own selves." (29)

Chart 4 – Scale of Differentiation

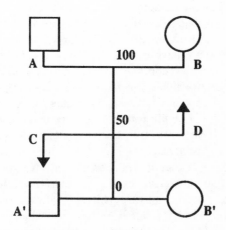

At the middle, symbiotic level, there is some degree of differentiation between the partners, and yet there is profound emotional interdependence. Here we see operating one of the laws of family systems—the principle of *homeostasis* — the tendency of the system to respond to any change with an effort (most often unconscious) to restore and return to balance. The family system will struggle to maintain its balance when change effects the system anywhere. If one of the partners begins to grow or develop through religious education, therapy or taking on new responsibilities, and if he/she begins to differentiate in new ways, the other partner is likely to *regress*. Why? The regression is an unconscious effort to try to preserve the homeostasis in the balance. That's why therapeutically it is important to work with the marital or family system as a whole. At the most differentiated level there ought to be some space, some separation between partners bound together by covenants for change to occur in the system and to allow children to grow in ways that move toward individuation.

Bowen's Scale of Differentiation provides the necessary link for conceptually relating family systems perspectives with the structural developmental account of stages of faith. In fact, structural developmental theories (including Piaget, Kohlberg, and Kegan, as well as Faith Development theory) provide a vital source for expanding and giving precision to Bowen and Friedman's use of the differentiation scale. *My intent here is to suggest that there are styles of family life and marital relation that correspond to differing stages of faith, and which represent places on the continuum from least to most differentiated family systems.* Chart 5 (see pages 114-115) introduces the hypothetical set of relations we see within these developmentally distinguishable styles of family life. Please understand that this model is based not on empirical enquiry and demonstration, at this point, but upon hypothetical theoretical construction, buttressed by informal observation.

Looking at Chart 5, note the categories of analysis that are to be found on the vertical left-hand column. These represent the "windows" or "lenses" of analysis of features of family system behavior. They include: Styles of Family Leadership and Followership; Styles of Decision-Making and Conflict Resolution; Styles of Family Discipline; Stages of Faith and Selfhood; and Images of God.

Across the top of Chart 5 you see the tentative names I have given to five developmentally different styles of family systems. I ask you to take these names not as pejorative or judgmental, but as efforts at description. I also ask you to recall what we said earlier about centripetal and centrifugal forces and phases in family life. This helps us remember that the same family on one day may exhibit some of the more individuated qualities, but on another day and in a critical time, it may manifest more of the legalistic or the symbiotic qualities. Under such circumstances there may be a reversion to earlier patterns. This means we can talk about optimal functioning and we can talk about crisis functioning, and we know that each of these types is likely to be to some degree present in any family system. Remember what Murray Bowen says: even the most mature and differentiated families get about a 70% on the differentiation scale. The Differentiated type on the far right of Chart 5, therefore, is probably an ideal to which we all aspire rather than something any of us has done much to attain.

Looking across the top of the chart we see Chaotic, Legalistic, Symbiotic, Individuating, and Differentiated types of family organization and functioning. Let's see if we can give some flesh to these by describing them briefly:

The Chaotic Family Style. You might think of a chaotic family as being characterized by parents or a parent who never had much parenting themselves. Sometimes such families are headed by teenage fathers and mothers, or one or the other, who take on the burdens and opportunities of parenting before having had the chance to individuate and become their own persons. This is not to say that all teenage parents or families are like this, but such families constitute an example of where one might expect to see chaotic structures. Leadership there tends to be arbitrary; it may be power-oriented, and above all you can expect it to be inconsistent. Decision-making in such a household is likely to be on the basis of whim and emotion, or to be impulsive or reactive. It is not necessarily the case that discipline will be physically and emotionally abusive, but if we remember this family style's inconsistency, it is likely to have some tendencies toward physical and emotional abuse.

In terms of stages of faith and selfhood, the operative level and style of faith would be close to the Intuitive-Projective stage with its impulsive selfhood. Images of God in this context would likely to be arbitrary, powerful and magical, with mixtures of an anthropomorphic and animistic or magical focus.

The Legalistic Family Style. This style of family functioning is frequently characteristic of fundamentalist families. There can be both Catholic and Protestant versions of the legalistic family style. These may be families where you have leaders who have had conversion experiences early in their lives, or may have had brokenness early in their lives, and in reconstructing have formed fairly rigid roles and role-expectations for family members. They have formulas for what parents should do, what fathers should do, what mothers should do, what children should be expected to do. These, typically, are described in fairly stereotypical roles. In such families there is typically a structure of dominance and a tendency to be authoritarian.

In terms of decision-making, there is an effort to follow the rules or established procedures, no matter what. There will be adherence to authoritarian teaching, an adherence to rules, even if conflict or hurt result. In such families there is some degree of insensitivity to emotional hurt. We understand this if we see that in the Mythic-Literal stage, with which this style corresponds, there is not yet a fully developed sense of the interiority of the self or an interiority of others. A reading of the "surfaces" of persons results from the lack of mutual interpersonal perspective taking. This means that reliance upon rules is crucially important and that following the rule is frequently more important than the consequences of rule adherence for the persons involved. The family leaders are so concerned about being "right" persons, or a "right" family, that they literally cannot see and feel what it is doing to the persons affected.[7]

In terms of discipline, this style manifests a reliance on moral reciprocity. If you do good you get rewarded, if you do wrong you get punished. It stresses obedience

Discipline:	• Physically and emotionally abusive	• Moral reciprocity • Legal point of view • Rules, reward, and punishment	• Emotional exclusion • Threat of isolation • Appeal to conscience	• Discussion and sanctions recognized as fitting, given constructive arguments and expectations • Age/stage appropriate virtues, emotions and sanctions	• Efforts at clarity about overall convenant
Stages of Faith & Selfhood:	• Intuitive — projective • Impulsive	• Mythic — Literal • Imperial	• Synthetic — conventional • Interpersonal • Institutinal	• Individuative — reflective • Inter-individual	• Conjunctive
Images of God:	• Arbitrary, powerful, magical • Mixed anthropomorphic and animistic focus	• Anthropomorphic • Sterna and just, but loving parent • External relation • Law giver	• Friend, life-line, companion, Spirit of harmony & protection of relations • Conscience and expectations • Internal relation	• Personal and beyond • Conceptual mediation • Conscious ideation • Connected consciously with aspects of experience and choices	• Paradoxical • Personal — systematic • Immanent — transcendent

These stages trail the personal development of partners because they require systems modifications — which take more time and may be blocked by relations in the extended family, or by the influence of immediate cultures or religious groups, or by uneveness of spousal development, or by critical events or circumstances, or some combinations of all of the above.

Chart 5 — Developmentally Related Styles of Family Systems

	Chaotic	Legalistic	Symbiotic	Individuating	Differentiated
Leadership:	• Arbitrary • Power-oriented • Inconsistent	• Stereo-typical roles • Structured dominance • Authoritarian	• Traditional expectations • Interpersonal sensitivities within clear roles • Unconscious controlling	• Separate roles & relationships • Some sense of family as system – shared responsibility for system • Conscious controlling	• Variegated, flexible, developmentally aware • Appreciates differences • Ecological perspective • No need for control
Decision-Making:	• Whim, emotion • Impulsive, reactive.	• Follow rules or established procedure • Authoritarian teaching • Adheres to rules even if causes conflict or hurt – insensitive to emotional hurt	• Find fit between intended or apprehended values • Conscious of group • If possible, avoid conflict – maintain relationship • Unconscious controlling	• Democratic expression of points of view • Expectations & traditions valued, but not determinative • Conflict minimized through discussion and generation of options • Consciously controlling	• Democratic when feasible • Participation according to multiple ability levels • No need to control

to the rules for the rules' sake, without much readiness to explain why the rules are important. There is a fear of chaos if the rules are not adhered to.

In terms of Stages of faith and selfhood this style correlates most explicitly with the Mythic-Literal stage and what Robert Kegan calls the Imperial style of selfhood.

Images of God favored by this family style would likely be anthropomorphic, a stern and just, but loving, parent. Such a God would be related to in external ways as a maintainer of justice and a law giver.

The Symbiotic Family Style. This family style exhibits a good deal more internal differentiation and interpersonal sensitivity. It likely places reliance upon traditional expectations regarding patterns of leadership, and has a fairly well-developed set of interpersonal sensitivities within clear roles. Here we get an unconsciously controlling style of family life. By this I mean that family leaders utilize the leverage of conventionally accepted role expectations and values to evoke conformity within the family.

In decision-making, there is an effort to find a fit between the intended or apprehended values the family espouses and the way members actually live. Members share a consciousness of the group and work at group maintenance. In symbiotic families every effort will be made to avoid conflict in order to maintain relationship. Rules adherence sometimes is subordinated to the maintenance of relationship.

In terms of discipline, the threat of emotional exclusion or of isolation is coupled with the appeal to conscience.

Favored images of God include thinking of God as a friend, a life-line, a companion, a spirit of harmony and protector of relationships. God, and the will of God are likely to be identified with conscience and expectations. Here we have an internal, personal, relationship with God.

The Individuating Family Style. In the individuating family style, we have a consistent leadership based upon reasonably separate roles and relationships. Among the adults and older (late adolescent or young adult) children there will be some awareness of the family *as a system*, with acceptance of shared responsibility for the health of the system. With this style we see a more conscious effort at control and governance.

Decision-making will involve democratic expression of points of view. This does not mean that everything is decided by majority vote. But it does mean that there is a democratic eliciting of the points of view of everybody before those who have the responsibility to make decisions do it. Everyone feels they are involved, and, at their level of maturity, responsible. As the family system matures you get closer to a true democracy. Expectations and traditions are valued, but are not strictly determinative. Conflict is minimalized through discussion and the generation of options, and a more conscious and shared kind of control becomes possible.

Discipline involves discussion and sanctions which are recognized as fitting. Reasons for rules are given, along with constructive arguments and expectations.

The Individuating style correlates with the Individuative-Reflective stage of faith. Images of God will be both personal and conceptual, and correlated with a fair amount of conscious and critically aware commitments.

Persons who enter parenting from one or another of these styles will experience the family life-cycle in radically different ways. As we try to work educationally, in ministry, and in family therapy with various family systems, it is very important to have some awareness of the characteristics of the family structural style with which we are working. It is not the case that everyone or every family has to get to the individuating stage. There are ways to be a genuinely Christian family within the patterns of any of these structural styles. But our work will be much more effective if we understand a family's structural style, with its characteristic strengths and limits, and enter into it, engaging it at the point of its developmental possibilities.

TOWARD A PRACTICAL THEOLOGY
OF FAMILY FAITH NURTURE

In the New Testament, especially in Luke and Paul, the family is placed under eschatological tension. In view of the inbreaking Kingdom of God, which is central in Jesus' preaching and teaching, the family, though of vital value as part of God's work of creation, can never be thought of as a final center of value. The family is not an end in itself. It is not a possession of the parents, nor the elders, nor the offspring. Rather, the family is a vital and changing trust in which we are called to faithful service in the human vocation to be in partnership with God. In Luke's Gospel, Jesus at twelve years of age sums up the essence of it: "Do you not know that I must be about my Father's service?" Yet, Jesus' "option for the children" in his teaching and praxis makes it clear that the family, as a context for the awakening and shaping of faith, is of crucial, penultimate importance.

Catholic Christians have placed tremendous emphasis upon the family, especially in the twentieth century. This concern has undergirded the strong objection to divorce, the prohibition of artificial birth control, and the strong stance against abortion on demand. One wonders, however, whether the passion for the family has been kept in the service of the eschatological vocation to anticipate and serve the Kingdom of God, or whether the principal concern, at points, has not been to augment the Catholic population.

Be that as it may, we have seen shifts in the ideals and patterns of Catholic Christian family life that seem to parallel the shifts in ecclesiology and theology of the laity from Vatican II. In terms of Chart 5, there has been a move from dominant images of the family clustered in the "Legalistic" and "Symbiotic" styles toward images taking form in the "Individuating" style. And of course, there have also been strong patterns of resistance to such changes.

Concurrent with—not because of—changes in the patterns of Catholic Christian family life, we have seen the family under increasingly severe stress and strain since the 1950s. I note the following trends:

1. The increased isolation of nuclear families due to mobility, geographical separation from extended families, and to the privatization of life in suburbia and in new urban settlements.
2. The disenfranchisement of parish and neighborhood structures of care and

accountability for families, due to the rise of reliance upon educational and mental health experts. These include, often tragically, recourse to methods of personal therapy that fail to work with clients in the context of their membership in families.

3. A casualness about divorce that suppresses awareness of the damage and disruptiveness it constitutes in the lives of the adults involved, as well as to children and extended families. (We do not need to exacerbate feelings of guilt and exclusion for divorced people. We *do* need better preparation for and support in marriage and family life.)

4. Cultural and societal changes in sex roles, sexual ethics, and standards. We see widespread confusion due to media saturation with sexually oriented messages in programming and advertising, and to the popular emergence of psychologies of self.

5. An epidemic of teen pregnancies and the expansion of an economic and social underclass subject to multiple patterns of addiction, exploitation, violence, and profound alienation. The most vulnerable victims of these conditions are the children of our common trust. We are producing faithless (those who have not experienced "good faith") generations in our cities and countryside.

In view of the foregoing, let us conclude with some thoughts about what we know and what we need to enact a practical theology of family faith nurture.

We know that the most powerful human influence on the forming faith of children is that exerted by parents' visible, consistent, and joyful living and expression of their own faith. In this society, where religion has tended to become the domain of women, the faith commitments of fathers have special salience. It is exciting how many fathers are increasingly proactive as mediators and nurturers of faith. Of course, mothers are crucial, as we have always known. But the father, particularly in this society, is an important index of whether that family system will have an overall sense of religious orientation and faith or not. Grandparents and relatives can be powerful supplements or, at times, substitutes in this process.

We know that involvement in parish life, led by parental presence and commitment, when joyfully inclusive of children and families, is essential to personal and family growth in faith. The family does not exist as an end in itself, as the parents' possession or justification. It is a vocational unit for partnership with God's work of creation, governance, and liberation-redemption.

We need to work out, in parishes and in family-clusters (Sawin 1979) a practical theology of the family in life-cycle developmental terms. This harkens back to an earlier point that we are undergoing a re-imaging of the Catholic family that parallels the theological shifts of the Second Vatican Council. There is a sense of exhilaration about this newness, coupled with a fair amount of dis-ease, wondering if we've left some essential baggage behind. One of the important tasks is to begin to sort out what of the tradition's family life baggage we must be sure we keep as we are nurturing more individuating families.

Let us consider some regions of ministry to and with families in Christian faith development. The following are particularly appropriate for offering through family life centers and parish programming:

* Christian LaMaze - working with parents in the anticipation of birth, particularly of their first child.
* Parenting Courses which involve active parenting, STEP-like programs, and faith development. 8 (Throughout we are concerned with learning new methods of child discipline, group decision-making, and the like, and how these affect faith life.)
* Intergenerational Bible study and sacramental preparation. This should include three-generational work with biblical materials in which we enact Bible stories and give children and adults chances to interact within the stories that are being offered. (White, 1988) Equally important is preparation for sacraments or understanding of sacraments in which they have already been involved. Such instruction, in communicating with children, also informs and deepens parents' understanding of what the sacraments are about.
* Courses in stepparenting and blended family leadership.
* Family Cursillo, Family Renew, Family Marriage Enrichment.
* Intergenerational Family Camping. Families can be clustered together. Singles can be included in family and family experiences.
* Divorce Recovery and Faith Development.

Then there are some important preventive and developmentally- oriented ministries we could initiate. For example:

* Begin involving children and youth (about 10th grade) in courses on family systems and the life cycle. After careful orientation to case studies and family systems theory, youth could observe (as though they were outsiders) the dynamics of their own families of origin, interviewing grandparents, parents and siblings.
* Teach parenting and family faith nurture as key elements in the vocation of Christians. This emphasis can be part of youth confirmation preparation and can be stressed in the mystagogia phase of the RCIA.
* Build family-like groups and activities for singles in parish and community.
* Develop a parish ecology of "family clusters."

There are therapeutic programs and initiatives we need to offer:

* Cooperative, interparish programs of accessible family therapy based, on life cycle, faith developmental, and family systems approaches.
* Therapy and growth groups for incest victims and their spouses. (One out of four American girls or women has experienced, or will experience, some form of sexual abuse or incestuous relationship. We have not yet begun to come to terms with how serious these problems are in our society, nor with how destructive they are, if not treated.)

Special ministries are needed with and to the chaotic end of the family styles continuum:

* Parenting courses for teen-aged mothers (and fathers, where available) can provide the context for more inclusive human and faith development processes, including nutrition and socialization training. (Belenky, 1-4, 8-9) Such courses can become wonderful opportunities for breaking the repetition of the chaotic family cycle.

* We need non-condemnatory group work on emotional and physical abuse, decision-making, conflict resolution, job skills, and vocational empowerment at the chaotic end of the spectrum.

The Church has a crucial role to play in public provision of and advocacy for faith forming and parenting training through Day-Care as we expand our offerings of those kinds of supports to families. (Fowler, Faith Development in Early Childhood)

CONCLUSION

I close this reflection on faith development through the family life cycle with an order of words that has become very important to me. It is an ancient prayer for families from the Episcopal Church's *Book of Common Prayer*.

> Almighty God, our heavenly Father, who settest the solitary in families: We commend to thy continual care the homes in which thy people dwell. Put far from them, we beseech thee, every root of bitterness, the desire of vainglory, and the pride of life. Fill them with faith, virtue, knowledge, temperance, patience, and godliness. Knit together in constant affection those who, in holy wedlock, have been made one flesh. Turn the hearts of the parents to the children, and the hearts of the children to the parents; and so enkindle fervent charity among us all, that we may evermore be kindly affectioned one to another; through Jesus Christ our Lord, AMEN.

ENDNOTES

[1] See the author's *Stages of Faith: The Psychology of Development and the Quest for Meaning* (San Francisco: Harper, 1981); Becoming Adult, Becoming Christian (San Francisco: Harper, 1984); and *Faith Development and Pastoral Care* (Philadelphia: Fortress, 1987).

[2] For extended descriptions of these stages see the sources included in the endnote above.

[3] For a detailed and nuanced account of the birth of faith and selfhood in this stage and the next see James W. Fowler, "Strength for the Journey: Early Childhood and the Development of Selfhood and Faith," *Faith Development and Early Childhood*, ed. Doris Blazer (Kansas City: Sheed, 1989).

[4] Vocation, as understood here, means the response we make with our total selves to God's call to partnership. It involves our work, our relationships, our private and public roles, and our use of our leisure. It is crucial to think of individuation in relation to vocation and with what our lives are for. See Fowler, *Becoming Adult, Becoming Christian*, Chapter 4.

[5] See Erik H. Erikson, *Childhood and Society* (New York: Norton, 1963); Daniel J. Levinson, et al., *The Seasons of a Man's Life* (New York: Knopf, 1978); and Anita Spencer, *Seasons: Women's Search For Self Through Life's Stages*

(New York: Paulist, 1982).
[6]For more on these different "voices of conscience" and their formation see
Thomas F. Green, "The Formation of Conscience in an Age of Technology,"
The John Dewey Lecture 1984 (Syracuse: Syracuse University). Can be
ordered from School of Education, 263 Huntington Hall, Syracuse
University, Syracuse, NY 13210.
[7]These characteristics are often found in what has come to be called "shame-bound
families." See Merle A. Fossum and Marilyn J. Mason, *Facing Shame:
Families in Recovery* (New York: Norton, 1986); and M. Scott Peck, M.D.,
People of the Lie (New York: Simon & Schuster, 1983).
[8]STEP stands for Systematic Training for Effective Parenting, a fine program by
Don Dinkmeyer and Gary D. McKay which nurtures family development in
the Individuating style. STEP is offered by the American Guidance Service,
Inc., Circle Pines, MN 55014.

WORKS CITED

Anderson, Herbert. *The Family and Pastoral Care*. Philadelphia: Fortress, 1984.
Belenky, Mary F, et.al. *Women's Ways of Knowing: The Development of Self,
Voice, and Mind*. New York: Basic, 1986, chapters 1-4, 8-9.
Brennan, Anne and Brewi, Janice. *Mid-Life Directions: Praying and Playing
Sources of New Dynamism*. Ramsey, NJ: Paulist, 1985.
Brueggemann, Walter. "Covenanting As Human Vocation," *Interpretation 33*
(1979), 115-129. See also James W. Fowler, Becoming Adult, Becoming
Christian (San Francisco: Harper, 1984), chapter 4.
Carter, Elizabeth A. and Monica McGoldrick, eds. *The Changing Family Life
Cycle*. Boston: Allyn, 1989.
Combrinck-Graham, Lee. "The Family Life Cycle and Families with Young
Children," *Clinical Implications of the Family Life Cycle*. Ed. James C.
Hansen and Howard A. Liddle. Aspen Systemps Corp, 1983.
Elkind, David. *The Hurried Child*. Reading MA: Addison-Wesley, 1981.
Friedman, Edward H. *Generation to Generation*. New York: Guilford, 1985.
Fowler, James W. "The Public Church As Ecology For Faith Nurture And
Advocate For Children." Ed Doris Blazer. *Faith Development in Early
Childhood*. Kansas City: Sheed, 1989.
———. "Perspectives on the Family from the Standpoint of Faith Development
Theory," Dallas, TX: *Perkins Journal*, Fall 1979.
Sawin, Margaret M. *Family Enrichment With Family Clusters*. Valley Forge:
Judson, 1979.
Straughn, Harold. *The 5 Divorces of a Healthy Marriage: Experiencing the Stages
of Love*. CBP, 1986.
White, James F. *Intergenerational Religious Education*. Birmingham: Religious
Education, 1988.
Whitmont, Edward C. *The Symbolic Quest: Basic Concepts of Analytical
Psychology*. Princeton: Princeton UP, 1978.

ADDITIONAL BIBLIOGRAPHY

Boszormenyi-Nagy, Ivan and Geraldine M. Spark. *Invisible Loyalties*. San Francisco: Harper, 1973.

Bowen, Murray. *Family Therapy in Clinical Practice*. New York: Aronson, 1978.

Demos, John. *Past, Present, and Personal: The Family and the Life Course in American History*. Cambridge: Oxford UP, 1986.

Fossum, Merle A., and Marilyn J. Mason. *Facing Shame: Families in Recovery*. New York: W. W. Norton, 1986.

Fowler, James W. *Stages of Faith*. San Francisco: Harper, 1981.

_____. *Becoming Adult, Becoming Christian*. San Francisco: Harper, 1984.

_____. *Faith Development and Pastoral Care*. Philadelphia: Fortress, 1987.

Friedman, Edwin H. *Generation to Generation*. New York: Guilford, 1985.

Hansen, James C. and Howard A. Liddle, eds. *Clinical Implications of the Family Life Cycle*. Aspen Systems Corporation, 1983.

Shorter, Edward. *The Making of the Modern Family*. New York: Basic/Harper, 1977.

Chapter Seven

THE SOCIAL MISSION OF THE FAMILY

James McGinnis and Kathleen McGinnis

As a family, we have felt the tension between involvement in social concerns and family life, especially as the children are getting older and their problems more complex. When they say, "When I try to talk to you, it seems like you're always thinking about something else" or "Why can't you come to my play next week?" we wonder whether we are shortchanging our children, at least at times, for our involvement in social concerns. What all of us are seeking is the sense of wholeness or harmony that is expressed by the Hebrew word *shalom*. This wholeness is also connoted in the term "family." We want the intimacy, trust, concern, security, and togetherness of shalom/family not only for our homes but also for our neighborhoods and our world. But most families do not see how they can do all three. And many other families feel threatened by the larger world and by all the changes they see around them. They see "family values" under attack in the violence, sexual permissiveness, and escalating rate of divorce in our society. Many also feel that family is being threatened by all the fuss about the roles of men and women in the home, society, and church and by what they see as the politicization or secularization of their church as it becomes more involved in social issues. They long for a return to "family values."

What are these values? Dolores Curran's list of fifteen traits of a healthy family closely resembles our own listing. "Togetherness" encompasses many of these values or traits—communication and listening; sharing; time together, especially around meals; play; family rituals and celebrations. Closely related is a second set that includes affection, affirmation, and support for each other. These values both imply and reinforce a deep respect of the family members for each other and for each person's individuality and need for privacy to complement the togetherness set of values. A third set might include a sense of responsibility, mutual trust, and a sense of right and wrong. Embodied in these general values is a call both to a deep sense of fidelity—fidelity between parent and child and, in marriage, fidelity between spouses ("in season and out of season," as Paul puts it)—and to a concern for others, especially relatives and neighbors. Finally, "family values" includes a religious core—a concern for prayer, for God.

While many families seem to feel that these values can be realized only in the security of retreating from the world, the thesis of this chapter is that family values are realized not only by "spending more time with the family" but also by participating as a family and with other families in the transformation of the world. To realize shalom in the home itself means addressing shalom at all levels of community—the home, the neighborhood, and the global community. Family community is built in part by participation in the building of neighborhood and global community.

More and more of our churches are seeing the educational task of parents as an outward-looking one:

> Their [parents'] role as educators is so decisive that scarcely anything can compensate for their failure in it. For it devolves on parents to create a family atmosphere so animated with love and reverence for God and [people] that a well-rounded personal and social development will be fostered among the children. Hence, the family is the first school of those social virtues which every society needs.
>
> ...It is through the family that they are gradually introduced into civic partnership with their fellow [human beings], and into the People of God. Let parents, then, clearly recognize how vital a truly Christian family is for the life and development of God's own people. (*Declaration on Christian Education* #3)

What this "civic partnership" and the "development of God's own people" are ultimately about is the transformation of the world and building the kingdom of God.

HOW SOCIETY AFFECTS THE FAMILY

Before we consider how the Christian family can participate in the transformation of society, it is necessary to examine in some detail the various ways in which the larger society affects family life and values. Modern society is proving to be both blessing and curse for families trying to live and share the gospel message. Urbanization and other characteristics of modern society have created a whole set of new social problems. This section will examine five such problems. These are not the only ones affecting Christian families today. They are, however, problems that impact families in a special way and problems that families have a special role in challenging. These five problems affect people in all societies and cultures to varying degrees, but they are particularly prevalent in the affluent West.

MATERIALISM

While modern capitalist and socialist economies have provided a more decent life in material terms for hundreds of millions of people, they have also created a very real problem for Christian families, and in capitalist societies the problem takes a special form. Pope Paul VI described it in specific terms:

> While very large areas of the population are unable to satisfy their primary needs, superfluous needs are ingeniously created. It can thus

rightly be asked if, in spite of all [our] conquests, [we are] not turning back against [ourselves] the results of [our] activity. Having rationally endeavored to control nature, [are we] not now becoming the slave[s] of the objects which [we make]? (*Octogesima Adveniens* #9)

"Slaves of the objects we make" describes the tendency in affluent societies for objects to become more important than persons. Objects are personified and persons are commodified. Even a cursory study of advertising reveals that objects provide us what persons are supposed to provide—identity, companionship, joy, intimacy. Persons are often treated as objects—sex objects, sales targets, units of labor. The effects of materialism—this commodification of the person—are particularly devastating on families.

More is better; happiness is having. Having things, having youth, having beauty becomes an all-consuming drive. Novelty becomes central—always getting something new. This drives takes a terrible toll on adults and children alike. The spiritual dimension of life is undermined, if not altogether lost. We seek recognition and affirmation in what we have rather than in who we are. Amassing swamps sharing. The more we seek security in money, goods, and huge insurance policies, the less we find our security in God and in each other. We are afraid to take risks for the gospel, for fear of their economic consequences. Fidelity to our spouse, our children, and our work becomes threatened as novelty is constantly dangled before us. This continual tantalizing of children as well as adults, of poor as well as rich, to get more things and to enjoy "the good life" threatens our very souls. No wonder the Roman Catholic bishops of Appalachia wrote in their pastoral letter, *This Land Is Home to Me*:

> Many times before outside forces have attacked the mountain's dream. But never before was the attack so strong. Now it comes with cable TV, satellite communication, giant ribbons of highway driving into the guts of the land. The attack wants to teach people that happiness is what you buy—in soaps and drinks, in gimmicks and gadgets, and that all of life is one big commodity market. It would be bad enough if the attack only tried to take the land, but it wants the soul, too. (Part I)

Writing off the have-nots. If happiness is having things, youth, and beauty, what happens to those who do not have these? These "have-nots"—the economically poor, the elderly, the disabled, the not-so-beautiful people of our society—are disregarded, disdained, discarded, and in some cases even destroyed.

Abusing the earth. The command of Genesis to subdue the earth calls us to be stewards of God's creation, to use the earth wisely, not to abuse its resources. But the prevailing "more is better" attitude is threatening the earth itself. We are all tempted by an attitude that says, "Who cares about future generations as long as I get mine."

A contrasting attitude, reverence for the earth as God's creation, leads to a reverence for persons, for future generations, and especially to reverence for the Creator. North American Indian parents have shared this value with their children for centuries, but it is an "endangered species" for many others in our materialistic world. This concern was prophetically addressed by a group of Canadian church leaders:

> In the final analysis what is required is nothing less than fundamental social change. Until we as society begin to change our own lifestyles based on wealth and comfort, until we begin to change the profit-oriented priorities of our industrial system, we will continue placing exorbitant demands on the limited supplies of energy in the North and end up exploiting the people of the North in order to get those resources...
>
> Ultimately, the challenge before us is a test of our faithfulness in the living God. For we believe that the struggle for justice and responsible stewardship in the North today, like that in distant Third World countries, is the voice of the Lord among us. We are called to involve ourselves in these struggles, to become active at the very center of human history where the great voice of God cries out for the fullness of life. (*Northern Development* #32, 34)

How families can respond to this appeal will be explored below.

INDIVIDUALISM

Closely related to materialism is the kind of individualism that is especially fostered in capitalist societies. This is not the individualism that pushes each person to do his or her best to see that personal needs are fulfilled, and to value personal freedoms. Rather, it is a consistent lifting up of self over all other considerations. One manifestation of this problem is a mentality that exalts possessions. A second manifestation is the separation of personal freedom from its social context. One Christian church's expression of this concern claims that we cannot adhere to a capitalism that

> exalts individual freedom by withdrawing it from every limitation, by stimulating it through exclusive seeking of interest and power, and by considering social solidarities as more or less automatic consequences of individual initiatives, not as an aim and a major criterion of the value of the social organization. (*Octogesima Adveniens* #26)

This lack of concern for the common good is partially a consequence of a third manifestation of individualism—the private property ethic as understood and practiced in our capitalist society. Private ownership entitles me to use my resources any way I want, says the culture. Not so, say Christian churches. For example:

> The recent Council [Vatican II] reminded us of this: "God intended the earth and all that it contains for the use of every human being and people. Thus, as all [persons] follow justice and unite in charity, created goods should abound for them on a reasonable basis." All other rights

whatsoever, including those of property and of free commerce, are to be subordinated to this principle....

In a word, "according to the traditional doctrine as found in the Fathers of the Church and the great theologians, the right to property must never be exercised to the detriment of the common good." (*Populorum Progressio* #22-23)

This kind of individualism weighs heavily on families. The highly competitive nature of our economic system and society, combined with the image of "rugged individuals raising themselves up by their own bootstraps," plus high mobility and an increase in nuclear and one-parent households, has isolated many families. This isolation has increased the need for material security, with the consequences thereof pointed out earlier. Children and adults alike see others as competitors—for grades, for jobs, for affection, for position, prestige, and power. Genuine Christian community becomes much more difficult. Supportive, noncompetitive relationships, even within families, become more difficult as competitive relationships permeate the society as a whole. The more that family members pursue personal goals to the detriment of the common good of family and society, the more it is that fractured and unhappy families seem to increase.

In public policy issues, materialism and individualism contribute to devastating situations. Governments and economic systems that permit inadequate wages, tolerate double-digit inflation, and allow high unemployment—in short, that do not guarantee the basic necessities of life to each person and family—place great burdens on families. Often both parents are forced to work long hours. Sometimes unemployed fathers are forced to leave their home if the other family members are to receive even minimal assistance. Unemployment—whether the cause is automation, multinational corporations closing factories for cheaper labor elsewhere, government budget cuts, or failure to plan and direct more capital to more job-creating industries—has its spiritual or psychological effects as well as physical and economic effects on workers and their families:

As lamentable as these financial costs are, the social and human impact is far more deplorable. In our society, persons without a job lose a key measure of their place in society and a source of individual fulfillment; they often feel that there is no productive role for them. Many minority youth may grow up without meaningful job experiences and come to accept a life of dependency. Unemployment frequently leads to higher rates of crime, drug addiction, and alcoholism. It is reflected in higher rates of mental illness as well as rising social tensions. The idleness, fear and financial insecurity resulting from unemployment can undermine confidence, erode family relationships, dull the spirit and destroy dreams and hopes. One can hardly bear to contemplate the disappointment of a family which has made the slow and painful climb up the economic ladder and has been pushed down once again into poverty and dependence by the loss of a job. (*The Economy: Human Dimensions* #12)

RACISM

The connection between the problems that families face in our society because of our economic system and the problem of racism is clearly pointed out in the U.S. Roman Catholic Bishops' pastoral letter on racism, *Brothers and Sisters to Us*:

> Racism and economic oppression are distinct but interrelated forces which dehumanize our society. Movement toward authentic justice demands a simultaneous attack on both evils. Our economic structures are undergoing fundamental changes which threaten to intensify social inequalities in our nation. We are entering an era characterized by limited resources, restricted job markets and dwindling revenues. In this atmosphere, the poor and racial minorities are being asked to bear the heaviest burden of the new economic pressures.... As economic pressures tighten, those people who are often black, Hispanic, Native American and Asian—and always poor—slip further into the unending cycle of poverty, deprivation, ignorance, disease, and crime.... The economic pressures exacerbate racism, particularly where poor white people are competing with minorities for limited job opportunities. (1-2)

The connection between materialism and individualism on the one hand and racism on the other is also noted in this pastoral letter. "Today's racism flourishes in the triumph of private concern over public responsibility, individual success over social commitment, and personal fulfillment over authentic compassion." *(Brothers and Sisters to Us* 6)

In terms of some specific facts of racism and their effects on families, unemployment among various minority groups in the United States is double (for Hispanic), triple (for black), and eight times (for Native Americans on reservations) that of white Americans. For minority youth, it is even worse.

Second, stereotypes of minority people continue to infect television, toys, movies, books, even school textbooks. The lack of positive self-image of minority people in these areas affects both children and adults in minority groups. Low self-esteem for many minority children and a superiority complex for many white children is one result.

Third, racism in education is manifested in lower teacher expectation for minority students; the lack of positive role models, either as staff members or resource people; the lack of decision-making power for minority people; situations where minority students predominate in remedial classes and whites in accelerated classes. Put very simply, racism in education means that minority students are shortchanged. They do not get the kind of education they need to prepare them psychologically and academically for adult life.

Last, the growing housing crisis that plagues minority families, coupled with the low self-esteem of many unemployed fathers in minority groups and the glaring lack of supportive service to minority families, has a devastating effect on these families.

SEXISM

Similar to racism in its dynamic is discrimination based on sex. The economic consequences of sexism are becoming more evident as more and more women join the work force because of economic need. Unequal pay for the same jobs and unequal access to more responsible and higher paying jobs often create serious problems for families where it is a woman's income that supports the family. For minority women there is double burden of discrimination.

The cultural consequences of sexism are perhaps less blatant but no less serious for families and thus for the society as a whole. Stereotypes of what it means to be a "man" and what it means to be a "woman" limit the emotional, physical, and spiritual development of men and women, boys and girls. For instance, nurturing and serving continue to be seen in most families as the woman's role. Often the result is females locked into service roles and males restricted in the development of the nurturing, service dimension of the whole person. As with racial stereotypes, sex-role stereotypes infect the books children and adults read, the toys children play with, and the ads, television shows, and movies we all see.

Another stereotype that has a profound effect on family life relates to what was said above about materialism. Friendships between men and women and marital fidelity are threatened as women (and sometimes men, too) are seen more and more as sex objects. This finds blatant expression in pornography and more subtle but pervasive expression in advertising, television, and movies. For example, women are told in many ways that it is their appearance that will get and hold their mate and bring them happiness.

VIOLENCE AND MILITARISM

Violence as a means of resolving conflicts, from interpersonal to international conflicts, does not seem to be decreasing. Military budgets in country after country continue to increase. The pursuit of security through bigger and better locks, police forces, prisons, armies, and nuclear warheads is growing.

This growing violence and militarism has a number of frightening consequences, for families and for society as a whole. Militarism as part of the national mentality manifests itself when schoolchildren in Michigan are recruited in a contest to design an insignia for a new Trident submarine, a "first strike" weapon with 408 nuclear warheads, each with destructive capacity of 2,040 Hiroshimas. A seven-year-old boy in Missouri is rewarded with a $20 bill for "drawing blood" (knocking a tooth out) from an opponent in a league football game. Spouse abuse and child abuse are especially frightening manifestations of the escalating violence in our society today.

Militarism affects families on the economic level as well. Some $300 billion in U.S. military expenditures for the fiscal year is a major reason why families cannot find adequate food, shelter, medical care, and education. "Demonic" and "an unparalleled waste of human and material resources" in the view of the World Council of Churches, (*Statement on Disarmament*) the arms race has also been described by the Vatican as "an act of aggression which amounts to a crime, for

even when they are not used, by their costs alone armaments kill the poor by
causing them to starve." (The Holy See on Disarmament)

FAMILY PARTICIPATION
IN THE CHURCH'S SOCIAL MISSION

THE SOCIAL MISSION OF THE CHURCH

To preach the gospel demands that we address these social problems. From a
Roman Catholic perspective, "action on behalf of justice and participation in the
transformation of the world fully appear to us as a constitutive dimension of the
preaching of the Gospel, or, in other words, of the Church's mission for the
redemption of the human race and its liberation from every oppressive situation."
(*Justice in the World* Introduction) In other words, it is not sufficient to care for the
victims of injustice—the corporal works of mercy. It is also necessary to work to
change the situations and structures (economic, political, cultural) that create the
victims in the first place—the works of justice.

"Family responsibilities" do not exclude families from participating in this
world-transforming task. In fact, Christian churches are explicitly challenging
families to participate:

> The family must also see to it that the virtues of which it is the teacher
> and guardian should be enshrined in laws and institutions. It is of the
> highest importance that families should together devote themselves
> directly and by common agreement to transforming the very structure of
> society. Otherwise, families will become the first victims of the evils that
> they will have watched idly and with indifference. (*Lineamenta: Role of
> the Christian Family* 44)

> It belongs to the laity, without waiting passively for orders and directives,
> to take the initiative freely and to infuse a Christian spirit into the
> mentality, customs, laws and structures of the community in which they
> live. (*Octogesima Adveniens* #48)

How Christian families specifically can be part of this mission will be
elaborated upon shortly. First, though, it is important to look at some of the
obstacles preventing families from participation and at a general strategy for
overcoming these obstacles.

OBSTACLES LIMITING FAMILY PARTICIPATION

The social context of family life presents a number of obstacles to families
participating in the church's social mission. Among these obstacles are the five
social problems identified earlier in the chapter. Other obstacles include a lack of
inspiration, lack of imagination, and lack of integration of the various aspects of
Christian living.

Faced with so many problems of their own, many families are not inspired to work with and for others. Economic insecurity and other fears keep them from the risks involved in social action. Often isolated from the victims of injustice, from people working for change, and from a supportive community, many families have just not been touched or moved to want to act.

Sometimes families are inspired to act, but do not know what to do. Lack of imagination and insight often keeps them from acting, especially when the social problems seem so complex and overwhelming. The more out of touch we are with the victims of injustice and with people working for change, the less imaginative as well as less courageous we are likely to be.

Lack of integration closely relates to this lack of imagination. Time is one dimension of this obstacle. Active Christian parents are among the most beleaguered of people—raising children, nurturing a marriage relationship or other supportive relationships in a home, being involved in school and church, trying to survive financially, actively participating in their neighborhood. Poor families and single-parent families generally have even less time and more sources of frustration. Unless parents can begin to see how to bring family life and social action together, they will never have time for both.

But more and more families are beginning to discover how their working in the world as a family community is enriching that family community. Generally, in this regard, parents are growing and learning right along with their children. Together, they are sharing their feelings about acting for justice. The time spent as a family to explain, choose, plan, and pray over family social actions fosters family community. Sometimes a parent and a child discover new dimensions of each other as persons and appreciate each other more in the process. The family deepens its sense of identity, significance, and pride by participating together in the church's social mission. And it is amazing how much of this mission can be expressed within the context of parenting.

Not that it always works out so neatly or that every family takes social mission so seriously all the time. For instance, on the ride back to Boston College from a visit to the Kennedy Library one summer, we were telling our children how important the witness of Robert Kennedy had been in shaping our own commitment and how inspirational the morning tour had been for us. Recalling how engaged they seemed to be in the tour as well, we asked the children what the highlight of the visit was for each of them. After some silence, David, age eleven, asked, "Does the lettuce and tomato on my sandwich count for my vegetable for lunch today?"

The other dimension of the lack of integration, besides time, is the dichotomy many people still experience between their personal spirituality and social action. Some Christians, parents included, do not participate in the church's social mission, because they do not see such participation as an essential expression of their faith. They do not recognize the call to transform the world as a call from Jesus. Instead, they often regard it as something for social activists and "secular humanists."

SOME COMPONENTS IN A STRATEGY
FOR OVERCOMING THESE OBSTACLES

The inspiration, imagination, and integration needed for the church's social mission to take root in one's heart will call for a conversion for many Christians. Among the components in this conversion process are the following three:

1. *Experiencing social ministry as a call from Jesus.* The more that the call to social ministry is seen as a call from Jesus, the more likely a person is to respond. Fostering a personal relationship with Jesus, especially through prayer and thoughtful reflection on the Scriptures, is essential. Parents doing this with their children, religious educators with their students, and ministries with parents and children can lead families to hear the voice of God:

> Is not this the sort of fast that pleases me
> —it is the Lord Yahweh who speaks—
> to bring unjust fetters
> and undo the thongs of the yoke,
> to let the oppressed to free,
> and break every yoke,
> to share your bread with the hungry,
> and shelter the homeless?
> (Isa. 58:6-7, JB)

> Blessed are those who hunger and thirst for righteousness....
> Blessed are the peacemakers. (Matt. 5:6, 9)

If we know more and more the Jesus who says this to us, walks with us as we follow his call, then we will be more willing to say yes.

The liturgical year retells the life of Jesus and thus his social mission. To make this mission explicit in the celebration of the liturgical year is essential in the conversion process. Advent and Christmas speak to us of God taking the world so seriously as to become human, of the coming of Jesus is simplicity to serve and not be served, of Jesus as the Prince of Peace. Lent marks the call to repentance for social sin as well as personal sin, the call to respond to Jesus as his passion is relived in the suffering of the hungry, the victims of racism and repression, the elderly, and so forth. Easter and Pentecost are the source of our hope and courage.

The Lord's Supper, together with baptism, expresses the charter, covenant-establishing even of Jesus' death-resurrection, by which we are incorporated into the covenant community. The Lord's Supper is God serving us, and it is our thankful response. In our responsive sacrifice, Calvin said, "are included all the duties of love." Radical self-giving should be the outcome... Receiving the Lord's Supper and living out the social implications of the Supper are one. Body broken "for the life of the world" (John 6:51) and blood "poured out for many" (Mark 14:24) carry cosmic, world-wide implications... Life itself must become the dynamic prolongation of the Lord's Supper. (Duba 18)

2. *Being touched by the victims and by advocates for justice.* As noted above, the victims of injustice as well as others working hard for justice can touch our hearts and move us to action. Their struggles and witness can help us overcome our complacency and fears.

3. *Being supported in community.* The support of others also helps us overcome our fears. Working with other families increased the effectiveness of our social action. Working with others provides both accountability and challenge. The example of others challenges us to live more faithfully. It is easier to run away, as it were, when no one else is around. Finally, working with other families often provides the necessary ingredient of enjoyment. Children especially need to enjoy social involvement if they are to integrate it into their own lives. Having other children along makes a real difference in many cases. And having other adults along also makes a real difference to parents, especially those who are parenting by themselves.

This was brought home to us several years ago when our oldest son, nine at the time, was adamant about not wanting to join us in serving a meal at a local soup kitchen and family shelter. He explained that his first experience there was difficult because some older children at the shelter were a lot tougher than he was. It was not until we stumbled onto the idea of having him invite a friend to go along that he was willing to return with us. Families that come together regularly to pray, play, or share in other ways sometimes evolve into groups that share economic resources and involve themselves more fully in the church's social mission. It is in such communities of families and other individuals that much of the hope for the church's social mission resides.

SPECIFIC WAYS FOR FAMILIES TO PARTICIPATE IN THE CHURCH'S SOCIAL MISSION

The suggestions that follow relate specifically to the five social problems identified earlier and are organized into three categories. First, they are life-style changes, those ways in which families can begin to live in ways and according to values different from those embodied in the culture. Second, there are the works of mercy by which families can respond to the immediate needs of people who are the victims of the materialism, individualism, racism, sexism, and violence in our society. Third, they are the works of justice, ways in which families can challenge the institutions or structures of society that embody anti-Christian values or whose policies cause or contribute to injustice. Part of this challenging of institutions is the creation of alternative institutions.

MATERIALISM AND INDIVIDUALISM

Living the alternative. Fidelity to another person, whether it is parent or children or married partners to one another, is a powerful sign in our age. This fidelity witnesses to commitment our novelty, to love and community over exploitation and individualism. Family can also be a living school of simplicity and stewardship. Involving the children in the family's recycling efforts is a basic way for all to care for the earth's resources. Economic sharing—whether it is families sharing tools or outgrown clothes or whether it is a community of families in which incomes are pooled and divided according to need—witnesses to the vision of gospel security and community spelled out The Acts of the Apostles. Stewardship and simplicity of heart also flow out of deep reverence for the earth. Family or community gardens, hiking, camping trips, a walk through the park with a child (when our own children were younger, such moments were few and far between) can all put us in touch with creation and the Creator. They provide opportunities to experience beauty and to learn to care for it.

Sharing our goods with the poor. For most families, their home is their most precious possession. Treating our home, as well as our other possessions, as a gift from God that is meant for service or sharing with the wider community is a significant way of making stewardship concrete for families. Opening our home to a person needing temporary or longer-term shelter—a teenager who cannot make it at home, an overnight traveler, and elderly relative, a foster child—is welcoming the Lord. If a family is able, emotionally as well as financially, to take someone else in, such a sharing of the home can have a deep impact on the children. They clearly participate daily in such an action.

Challenging institutions that encourage materialism and individualism. Because one crucial source of materialism and selfish individualism is advertising, an important task for parents and teachers is to help children become conscious and critical of who they are manipulated by advertising, packaging, and the other ways they are being urged to buy things. Television advertising is especially troublesome. Watching commercials with children and pointing out or asking them to point out some of the techniques being used is a first step for parents. Further, corporate sponsors and the media need to hear the prophetic voice of Christian families. Family letters are one possibility. Families have participated in consumer boycotts of corporations pursuing maximization of profit at the expense of people. Sometimes, though, parents need to check out whether their children really understand what the issue is. We overheard our son Tom, age ten at the time, explaining to a friend why our family was participating in the boycott of Nestle products: "They [Nestle] put infant formula in their candy bars and that makes poor babies sick."

Supporting alternative institutions that do not exploit people or the earth is another approach. Thus, many families buy their fruits and vegetables directly from small farmers or are part of a local food cooperative, as an alternative to the growing control over North American food production by giant agribusiness corporations. Church or neighborhood credit unions offer families and others an alternative to commercial banks that sometimes write off poorer neighborhoods.

RACISM

Living the alternative. The development of healthy racial attitudes in children and assisting children to experience and desire a more multicultural and multiracial world are an important dimension of the family's social mission. Because the home environment is so crucial in the formation of racial attitudes, families should focus there first. Do the visuals—so important in early learning—in the home (pictures, magazines, toys, books) portray a variety of peoples and cultures?

As we look at the wider environment, we see important experiences that shape racial attitude. Are neighborhood, school, church, and shopping center multicultural or mono-cultural environments? If the people who provide important services for the family, such as teachers and physicians, are all white, then children are learning that only white people do important things. If wider environment is mono-cultural, it is more difficult to provide children and adults with those experiences—contracts, friendships—that promote respect and appreciation for people of all races and cultures.

Challenging institutions perpetuating racial stereotypes. Institutions help shape attitudes. Thus, we need to do more than provide multicultural books and toys for our children to offset those which portray only white characters or portray minority characters in stereotypical ways. Parents need to provide more racially accurate toys and to remove toys that are racially offensive. Teachers, curriculum developers, and textbook publishers can all be encouraged to find or develop multicultural materials.

SEXISM

Living the alternative. At the level of the individual family, there are as many ways of dealing with the sex-role stereotypes as there are with racial stereotyping. In families where there are both male and female role models, more equitable sharing of household tasks could be encouraged. In single-parent homes, by necessity, this kind of non-stereotyped modelling often is the practice. All parents can be careful about the kinds of messages they give children about what are "appropriate" tasks for men and women. Similarly, parents can and should promote a diversity of physical, intellectual, and artistic capabilities in their children. Many societies continue to limit such diversity, for both girls and boys, but especially for girls. Parents also need to concern themselves with internal qualities in their children. That is, caring, nurturing, and sensitive qualities are as important for boys as for girls. Assertive, independent, decisive, inventive qualities are as important for girls as for boys.

Challenging institutions perpetuating sex-role stereotypes. Unfortunately, sexism as well as racism permeate many of our schools. Parents can challenge sexism in the curriculum by urging schools to examine their instructional materials and to supplement the materials that fail adequately to present nonsexist images and the contributions of women to the world. As with racial stereotyping, toys, books, and the media are an important focus of family action. Sexism in our churches also needs to be challenged. Children as well as adults can work for greater participation for women of all ages in church functions and leadership positions.

VIOLENCE AND MILITARISM

Living the alternative. The development of nonviolent and cooperative attitudes and skills in children is an important responsibility of parents and a way by which families can help create alternative attitudes and models in regard to the prevailing violence in our society. This responsibility can be exercised in a variety of ways. First, parents can create an affirming, cooperative, accepting environment in which nonviolent attitudes and skills are nurtured. Affirmation also encourages social involvement. No adult or child gets involved in social action for very long without a sense of self-worth or self-confidence. When risks are involved—even such things as "What will the other kids think?"—it is the people who feel good about themselves who can stand up for their beliefs.

A cooperative environment is also essential, as violence is nurtured by excessive competition. Family chores can be structured in such a way that they will involve persons working together. Cooperative games can balance competitive games. But even with our emphasis on fun in sports rather than just winning, our ten-year-old daughter was hesitant to enter a community "fun run" unless there was a trophy at the end. Family prayer contributes as well, especially when leadership is shared among all family members. Stewardship of our talents—sharing them with family members and others—promotes this cooperative spirit and environment.

An accepting, forgiving environment does much to reduce tension, diffuse resentment, and thereby promote nonviolent ways of dealing with conflict. One necessary ingredient for such an environment is for parents to feel good about themselves and their relationships. For couples, the essential harmony of marital love is both nurtured by and nurturing of acceptance and forgiveness within the family.

In all these ways, families create that love described by Paul in the letter to the Ephesians:

> If we live by the truth and in love, we shall grow in all ways into Christ, who is the head by whom the whole body is fitted and jointed together, every joint adding its own strength, for each separate part to work according to its function. So the body grows until it has built itself up, in love. (Eph. 4:15-16, JB)

> Be subject to one another out of reverence for Christ. (Eph. 5:21)

Where this is an environment of affirmation, cooperation, and acceptance, parents can convey to their children the attitudes, values, and skills of nonviolence. The skills include basic communication and conflict resolution skills that can generate alternative solutions in conflict situations. The promotion of regular family meetings or councils is one way of structuring such nonviolent conflict resolution into family life. Developing alternatives to violent (psychological as well as physical) forms of discipline is also crucial. The more violence is used on children, the more violence will be used by children.

Challenging institutions that promote violence. As we pointed out with regard to materialism, the media is an important institution on which to focus family action. Violence on television—in cartoons as well as in many prime time shows—has a negative effect on children. Besides challenging the extent of such programming, parents can spend time with their children talking over the violence they do encounter on television. This is also true of actual violence in the world, whether experienced in the neighborhood or seen on the news.

There are at least two approaches that families can take to challenge the growing militarism in our society. The first is more indirect. Instead of the "us against them" attitudes on which militarism thrives, we can educate ourselves and our children to the global nature of God's family. Pairing with, as well as praying for, sisters and brothers in other parts of the world can put us personally in touch with this global reality. Individual families as well as congregations have paired with families and congregations in other countries. Here, again, the kinds of artifacts, magazines, and people that come into our homes help shape our attitudes and the breadth of our awareness.

In these and other ways, families can help promote a sense of patriotism that is consistent with the gospel and does not pit one people or nation against another. A Roman Catholic expression of such patriotism is reflected in the following passage from Vatican II:

> Citizens should develop a generous and loyal devotion to their country, but without any narrowing of mind. In other words, they must always look simultaneously to the welfare of the whole human family, which is tied together by the manifold bonds linking races, peoples, and nations. (*Gaudiem et Spes* #75)

At the same time that parents foster a sense of global awareness in their children, they can also undertake more direct challenges of institutions fostering militarism. Family letters to political representatives on the need to reverse the arms race is one step. Tax resistance is still illegal and therefore risky and beyond most of us. Nevertheless, it can be seen to be implied in the church's teaching on noncooperation with evil. Families need help in facing this issue. Some parents have taken such steps, if only symbolically, and have involved their children in the process. Other families have participated in public demonstrations to give prophetic witness for gospel values and against specific expressions of what they consider to be an immoral militarism.

CONCLUSION: A RETURN TO FAMILY VALUES

While most families would not consider some of the above actions and activities as part of family life, more and more families are coming to see that the gospel of Jesus asks such radical stances from his followers. Those families who are beginning to see this and who are supported in their response by a Christian community are bearing witness to the rest of us to be willing to risk for the gospel. It is clear from church teaching that families have a definite responsibility to address these pressing social problems that cause injustice, threaten human life and dignity, and undermine family life itself. In so doing, each family, as one among many families in the world, find fulfillment in service to others.

But it is not only the "concern for others" aspect of the list of family values that is realized in this understanding of family participation in the church's social mission. All the other family values are realized as well:

* The "togetherness" set of values if furthered by all the suggestions above on living the alternative to violence, especially the communication and conflict resolution skills and the family meeting; by the simplicity/stewardship suggestions involving sharing of talents and alternative celebrations that focus on people rather than things; and by the family's developing a sense of common mission and one they experience with other families.
* The affirmation and mutual support values are promoted by the centrality of peacemaking in the home itself—again, all the suggestions on living the alternative to violence. Challenging sex-role stereotypes and racial stereotypes affirms and promotes the full human development of each family member. Working with other families, encouraging risk-taking, and supporting one another in actions of all kinds also promote these family values.
* Family members' sense of responsibility and sense of right and wrong are furthered by shared decision-making through the family and the implementation of such decisions. The stewardship suggestions on caring for the earth and for future generations as well as sharing talents with family members and other nurture a deep sense of responsibility. Discussing social problems, encouraging one another to form opinions and stand up for what each believes—all promote these family values.
* The family value of concern for God, the gospel, and prayer is central to the whole vision of family life articulated in this chapter. It is Jesus who calls family members to participate in actions that build up the whole body of Christ. It is the resurrection of Jesus that gives family members the hope that if they die to themselves in embracing one another for life and embracing a suffering world, their seeds will bear much fruit. It is the spirit of Jesus—encountered in contemplation, action, and in coming together prayerfully with others—that inspires and gives family members the courage to take the risks necessary to build shalom/family/community—the family community, the neighborhood community, and the global community.

WORKS CITED

Curran, Dolores. *Traits of a Healthy Family*. San Francisco: Winston, 1983.

"Declaration on Christian Education". *The Documents of Vatican II*. New York: Guild, 1966.

Duba, Arlo D. "Theological Dimensions of the Lord's Supper." Quoted in *Educational Ministry of the Presbyterian Church* (U.S.A.). From *Worship in the Community of Faith*. Ed. Harold M. Daniels. Joint Office of Worship, Presbyterian Church (U.S.A.), 1982.

Gaudium et Spes. *The Documents of Vatican II*. Ed. Walter M. Abbot. New York: America, 1966.

The Holy See on Disarmament (1976). *To Proclaim Peace: Religious Statements on the Arms Race.* Ed. John Donaghy. Nyack, N.Y.: Fellowship of Reconciliation, 1981.

Lineamenta: The Role of the Christian Family in the Modern World. Washington: USCC, 1979.

NCCB. *The Economy: Human Dimensions. Renewing the Earth: Catholic Documents on Peace, Justice and Liberation.* Garden City: Doubleday, 1977.

———. *Brothers and Sisters to Us.* Washington: USCC, 1979.

Northern Development: At What Cost? Ottawa: Canadian Catholic Conference, 1975.

Pope Paul VI. *Octogesima Adveniens. Renewing the Earth: Catholic Documents on Peace, Justice and Liberation.* Garden City: Doubleday, 1977.

———. *Populorum Progressio. Renewing the Earth: Catholic Documents on Peace, Justice and Liberation.* Garden City: Doubleday, 1977.

Statement of the World Council of Churches Conference on Disarmament. Glion, Switzerland, April 9-15, 1978. *Peacemaking: The Believers' Calling.* United Presbyterian Church U.S.A.

Synod of Roman Catholic Bishops. *Justice in the World. Renewing the Earth: Catholic Documents on Peace, Justice and Liberation.* Garden City: Doubleday, 1977.

This Land Is Home to Me. Renewing the Earth: Catholic Documents on Peace, Justice and Liberation. Garden City: Doubleday, 1977.

Appendix

RESOURCE GUIDE ON FAITH GROWTH AND TRANSMISSION IN FAMILIES

Dolores T. Waters

The following resource guide contains selected books, studies, articles, special publications, and resources compiled for use by pastoral and educational ministers in their work with families through the life cycle. It is focused on resources to assist ministers and families in nurturing the faith journey of the family and in empowering families to share the values and teachings of our rich heritage as Catholic Christians. The resource guide is developed using the major headings from the foundational principles in Chapter 1.

THE IDENTITY AND MISSION OF THE CATHOLIC FAMILY

John Paul II. *Familiaris Consortio. Papal Exhortation on the Family.* Washington, DC: USCC OPPS, 1981.

NCCB. *A Family Perspective in Church and Society.* Washington, DC: USCC, 1988.

NCCB. *Families at the Center—A Handbook for Parish Ministry with a Family Perspective.* Washington, DC: USCC, 1990

Special Feature: The Christian Family. Living Light 18.1 (Spring 1981).

Thomas, David. "Home Fires: Theological Reflections." *The Changing Family.* Ed. Saxton, et al. Chicago: Loyola University, 1984.

USCC, Commission on Marriage and Family Life. *A Positive Vision for Family Life: A Resource Guide for Pope John II's Apostolic Exhortation Familiaris Consortio.* Washington, DC: USCC OPPS, 1985.

USCC, Commission on Marriage and Family Life. *Families in the '80's: Family Decade Resource for the Community, Diocese and Parish.* Washington, DC: USCC, 1980.

USCC, Commission on Marriage and Family Life. *Parish Family Ministry Resources.* Washington, DC: USCC, 1980.

USCC, Department of Education. *Parenting and Family Education: A Planning and Discussion Guide.* Washington, DC: USCC, 1979.

Vatican. *Charter of the Rights of the Family.* Washington, DC: USCC OPPS, 1983.

THE FAMILY AS A SYSTEM GROWING OVER TIME

Anderson, Herbert. *The Family and Pastoral Care*. Philadelphia: Fortress, 1984.

Bradshaw, John. *Bradshaw on the Family*. Deerfield: Health Communications, Inc., 1988.

Carter, E.A. and M. McGoldrick. *The Changing Family Life Cycle*. Boston: Allyn & Bacon, 1989.

Curran, Dolores. *Traits of the Healthy Family*. San Francisco: Harper and New York: Ballatine Books, 1983.

Curran, Dolores. *Stress and the Healthy Family*. San Francisco: Harper, 1985.

Durkin, Mary G. *Making Your Family Work*. Chicago: Thomas More, 1988.

Elkind, David. *The Hurried Child*. Reading: Addison-Wesley, 1981.

Elkind, David. *All Grown-Up and No Place to Go*. Reading: Addison-Wesley, 1983.

Friedman, Edwin H. *Generation to Generation: Family Process in the Church and Synagogue*. New York: The Guilford, 1985.

Galinsky, Ellen. *The Six Stages of Parenthood*. Reading: Addison-Wesley, 1987.

Napier, Augustus with Carl Whitaker. *The Family Crucible*. New York: Harper, 1978.

Pearsall, Paul. *The Power of the Family—Strength, Comfort and Healing*. New York: Doubleday, 1990.

Power, Thomas A. *Family Matters — A Layman's Guide to Family Functioning*. Meredith, NH: Hathaway, 1989.

Satir, Virginia. *Peoplemaking*. Palo Alto: Science and Behavior Books, Inc., 1972.

Steinburg, Lawrence D. *Understanding Families with Young Adolescents*. Carboro: Center for Early Adolescence, 1980.

Stinnett, Nick and John DeFrain. *Secrets of Strong Families*. Boston: Little, Brown, and Co., 1985.

Stinnett, Nick, et. al., eds. *Family Strengths*. Lincoln: University of Nebraska, 1982.

Strommen, Merton and Irene. *Five Cries of Parents*. San Francisco: Harper, 1985.

THE FAMILY AND ETHNICITY

Augsberger, David. "Family, Family Theory, and Theraphy Across Cultures. *Pastoral Counseling Across Cultures*. Philadelphia: Westminster, 1986.

Billingsley, Andrew. *Black Families in White America*. (20th Anniversary Edition) New York: Simon and Schuster, 1968.

Bowman FSPA, Thea, editor. *Families: Black and Catholic, Catholic and Black*. Washington, DC: USCC, 1985.

Deck, Allan Figueroa. *The Second Wave — Hispanic Ministry and the Evangelization of Cultures*. New York: Paulist, 1989.

Faith and Culture: A Multicultural Catechetical Resource. Washington, DC: USCC, OPPS, 1987.

Foster, Charles, editor. *Ethnicity in the Education of the Church*. Nashville: Scarritt, 1987.

McGoldrick, Monica. "Ethnicity and the Family Life Cycle." *The Changing Family Life Cycle*. Boston: Allyn & Bacon, 1989.

McGoldrick, M., J. K. Pearce, and J. Giordano. *Ethnicity and Family Therapy*. New York: Guilford, 1982.

NCCB. *The Hispanic Presence: Challenge and Commitment*. Washington, DC: USCC OPPS, 1983.

Roberts, J. Deotis. *Roots of a Black Future: Families and Church*. Philadelphia: Westminster, 1980.

Smith, Wallace Charles. *A Family Enrichment Curriculum for the Black Church*. Ann Arbor, MI: University Microfilms International, 1979.

THE FAMILY AND SOCIETY

Bellah, R.N., R. Masden, W.M. Sullivan, A. Swidler and S. M. Tipton. *Habits of the Heart: Individualism and Commitment in the American Life*. Berkeley: University of California, 1985.

Brigham, Frederick H., Jr. and Steven Priester, eds. *Families, The Economy and the Church: A Book of Readings and Discussion Guide*. Washington, DC: USCC OPPS, 1986.

Edelman, Marian Wright. *Families in Peril — An Agenda for Social Change*. Cambridge: Harvard University, 1987.

Family Research Council of America. *Cultural Trends and the American Family*. Washington, DC: Family Research Network Conference, 1986.

Foster, Charles. "The Changing American Family." *Religious Education as Social Transformation*. Ed. Allen J. Moore. Birmingham: Religious Education.

Gallup, George and Castelli, Jim. *The American Catholic People*. Garden City: Doubleday, 1987.

Gallup, George and Castelli, Jim. *The People's Religion: American Faith in the 90's*. New York: Macmillan Company, 1990.

Hochschild, Arlie with Anne Machung. *The Second Shift — Working Parents and the Revolution at Home*. New York: Viking, 1989.

Levitan, Sar A., Richard S. Belous, and Frank Gallo. *What's Happening to the American Family — Tensions, Hopes, Realities*. Baltimore: Johns Hopkins, 1988.

Kenniston, Kenneth and The Carnegie Council on Children. *All Our Children: The American Family Under Pressure*. New York: Harcourt Brace Jovanovich, 1977.

FAMILIES AS THE PRIMARY CONTEXT FOR FAITH GROWTH

Blazer, Doris, editor. *Faith Development in Early Childhood*. Kansas City: Sheed And Ward, 1989.

Cavalletti, Sofia. *The Religious Potential of the Child*. New York: Paulist, 1983.

Chamberlain, Gary. *Fostering Faith — A Minister's Guide to Faith Development*. New York: Paulist, 1988.

Curran, Dolores. *Family: A Church Challenge for the 80's*. Minneapolis, MN.: Winston, 1980.

Durka, Gloria and Joan Marie Smith, eds. *Family Ministry*. Minneapolis: Winston, 1980.

Dykstra, Craig and Sharon Parks. *Faith Development and Fowler*. Birmingham: Religious Education, 1987.

Dykstra, Craig. *Vision and Character*. New York: Paulist, 1981.

Finley, Kathy and Mitch. *Christian Families in the Real World*. Chicago: Thomas More, 1984.

Fowler, James W. *Stages of Faith: The Psychology of Human Development and the Quest for Meaning*. San Francisco: Harper, 1981.

Fowler, James. *Becoming Adult, Becoming Christian*. San Francisco: Harper, 1984.

Fowler, James. *Faith Development and Pastoral Care*. Philadelphia: Fortress, 1987.

Gardner, Freda A. and Carol Rose Ikeler. *Active Parenting in the Faith Community*. Atlanta: Presbyterian Publishing House. [Popkin, Michael. *Active Parenting: Teaching Cooperation, Courage and Responsibility*. San Francisco: Harper, 1987.]

Greeley, Andrew. *The Religious Imagination*. New York: Sadlier, 1981.

Greeley, Andrew M. *The Young Catholic Family: Religious Images and Marriage Fulfillment*. Chicago, IL: The Thomas More, 1980.

Guernsey, D. *A New Design for Family Ministry*. Elgin, IL: David Cook Publisher Co., 1982.

Hater, Robert J. *Holy Family — Christian Families in a Changing World*. Allen: Tabor, 1988.

Larson, Jim. *Growing a Healthy Family — How to Be Christian Parents in a Stress-Filled Time*. Minneapolis: Augsburg, 1986.

Larson, Jim. *A Church Guide for Strengthening Families — Strategies, Models, Programs, and Resources*. Minneapolis: Augsburg, 1984.

Lee, James Michael, editor. *Handbook of Faith*. Birmingham: Religious Education, 1990.

Martin, Thomsas. *Christian Family Values*. New York: Paulist, 1989.

NACDFLM. *Family Spirituality: The Sacred in the Ordinary*. National Association of Catholic Diocesan Family Life Ministers, 1984.

Parks, Sharon. *The Critical Years: The Young Adult Search for a Faith to Live By*. San Francisco: Harper, 1986.

Patton, John and Brian H. Childs. *Christian Marriage and Family - Caring for Our Generations*. Nashville: Abingdon, 1988.

Roloff, Marvin L. *Education for Christian Living*. Minneapolis, MN.: Augsburg Publishing House, 1987.

Sawyers, Lindell, ed. *Faith and Families*. Philadelphia: The Geneva, 1986.

Saxton, Stanley L., P. Voydanoff, A.A. Zukowski, eds. *Family: Reflections on Familiaris Consortio*. Chicago: Loyola University, 1984.

Schulman, Michael and Eva Mekler. *Bringing Up a Moral Child: A New Approach for Teaching Your Child to be Kind, Just, and Responsible*.

Reading: Addison-Wesley, 1985.

Sheek, G. William. *The Word on Families — A Biblical Guide to Family Well-Being*. Nashville: Abingdon, 1985.

Thomas, David M. *Family Life and the Church: A Manual for Leaders and Participants*. New York: Paulist, 1979.

Westerhoff, John. *Living the Faith Community — The Church That Makes a Difference*. San Francisco: Harper, 1985.

FAMILY FAITH GROWTH AND TRANSMISSION: RITUAL AND LITURGY

Collins OSB, Mary. *Worship: Renewal to Practice*. Washington, DC: Pastoral, 1987.

Cunningham, Nancy Brady. *Feeding the Spirit — How to Create Your Own Ceremonial Rites, Festivals, and Celebrations*. San Jose: Resource Publications, 1988.

DeGidio, Sandra. *Enriching Faith through Family Celebrations*. Mystic: Twenty-Third Publications, 1989.

Dunn, Frank Gasque. *Building Faith in Families — Using the Sacraments in Pastoral Ministry*. Wilton: Morehouse-Barlow, 1986.

Empereur S.J., James. *Worship: Exploring the Sacred*. Washington, DC: Pastoral, 1987.

Hock, Mary Isabelle. *Worship through the Seasons*. San Jose: Resource Publications, 1987.

Marchal, Michael. *Adapting the Liturgy — Creative Ideas for the Church Year*. San Jose: Resource Publications, 1989.

Nelson, Gertrud Mueller. *To Dance with God — Family Ritual and Community Celebration*. New York: Paulist, 1986.

Weil, Louis. "Facilitating Growth in Faith through Liturgical Worship." *Handbook of Faith*. Ed. James Michael Lee. Birmingham: Religious Education, 1990.

Westerhoff, John. *Learning through Liturgy*. New York: Seabury, 1978.

Westerhoff, John and William Willimon. *Liturgy & Learning through the Life Cycle*. New York: Seabury, 1980.

Westerhoff, John. "Catechetics and Liturgics." *PACE 19* (February 1990).

Wilde, James, editor. *At That Time — Cycles and Seasons in the Life of a Christian*. Chicago: Liturgy Training Publications, 1989.

FAMILY FAITH GROWTH AND TRANSMISSION: RELIGIOUS EDUCATION/CATECHESIS

Benson, Peter, Dorothy Williams, Carolyn Eklin and David Shuller. *Effective Christian Education: A National Study of Protestant Congregations*. Minneapolis: Search Institute, 1990.

Benson, Peter, and Carolyn Eklin. *Effective Christian Education: A National Study of Protestant Congregations — A Summary Report on Faith, Loyalty, and Congregational Life*. Minneapolis: Search Institute, 1990.

Chesto, Kathleen O'Connell. *Family Centered Intergenerational Religious Education*. Kansas City: Sheed and Ward, 1988. [Includes Director's Guide, Year 1 and Year 2 programs]

Daglish, William A. *The Family Centered Model*. Nashville: Division of Education, United Methodist Board of Discipleship, 1974.

Daglish, William A. Ph.D. *Models for Catechetical Ministry in the Rural Parish*. Washington, DC: National Conference of Diocesan Directors of Religious Education, 1982.

DeBoy, James, Regis Krusniewski, Jeannette Suflita, and Charles Cassetta. *Partners in Catechesis — Family and Catechists*. Dubuque: Wm. C. Brown, 1984.

DeGidio, Sandra. *Sharing Faith in the Family*. Mystic: Twenty-Third Publications, 1981.

Faith and Culture: A Multicultural Catechetical Resource. Washington, DC: USCC, OPPS, 1987.

Foster, Charles, editor. *Ethnicity in the Education of the Church*. Nashville: Scarritt, 1987.

Griggs, Donald and Patricia. *Generations Learning Together: Learning Activities for Integenerational Groups in the Church*. Nashville: Abingdon, 1980.

Iannone, Joseph and Mercedes. "The Educational Ministry of the Christian Family." *Living Light* 21.2 (January 1985).

Kelly, Frank, Peter Benson, and Michael Donahue. *Toward Effective Parish Religious Education for Children and Young People*. Washington, DC: NCEA, 1986.

Kitchen Table Gospel — An Adventure in Family Catechesis. Granada Hills, CA: Sandalprints Publishing, 1990. [Lectionary-based, home-driven catechetical program.]

Lee, James Michael. "Facilitating Growth in Faith through Religious Instruction." *Handbook of Faith*. Ed. James Michael Lee. Birmingham: Religious Education, 1990.

Parenting and Religious Education. Religious Education 83.4 (Fall 1988).

Purcell, Antionette, and Martin Weithman. *Developing a Parish Plan for Family Catechesis*. Washington, DC: NCCD, 1989.

Purnell, D. *Working with Families*. Rochester, NY: Family Clustering, Inc., 1980.

Sawin, Margaret. M. *Family Enrichment with Family Clusters*. Valley Forge: Judson, 1979.

Sawin, M. ed. *Hope for Families: Stories of Family Clusters in Diverse Settings*. New York: Sadlier, 1982.

USCC, Department of Education. *Family-Centered Catechesis: Guidelines and Resources*. Washington, DC: USCC, 1979.

White, James F. *Intergenerational Religious Education*. Birmingham: Religious Education, 1988.

FAMILY FAITH GROWTH AND TRANSMISSION: SOCIAL INVOLVEMENT

Condon, Camy and James McGinnis. *Helping Kids Care — Harmony Building Activities for Home, Church, and School.* St. Louis: Institute for Peace and Justice and Meyer Stone Books, 1989.

McGinnis, Jim. *Helping Families Care.* St. Louis: Institute for Peace and Justice and Meyer Stone Books, 1989.

McGinnis, Jim, editor. *Partners in Peacemaking — Family Workshop Models Guidebook for Leaders.* St. Louis: Institute for Peace and Justice, 1984.

McGinnis, Jim and Kathleen. *Building Shalom Families: Christian Parenting for Peace and Justice.* St. Louis: Institute for Peace and Justice, 1986. [Complete video package containing: two 120-minute VHS videotapes, 32-page guidebook, Parenting for Peace and Justice book, and worksheets and action brochures.]

McGinnis, Jim and Kathleen. *Parenting for Peace and Justice — Ten Years Later.* Maryknoll: Orbis Books, 1990.

McGinnis, Kathleen. *Starting Out Right — Nurturing Young Children as Peacemakers.* St. Louis: Institute for Peace and Justice and Meyer Stone Books, 1989.

Nelson, Randolph. "Facilitating Growth in Faith through Social Ministry." *Handbook of Faith.* Ed. James Michael Lee. Birmingham: Religious Education, 1990.